9/03

27.45

The Thirteen Colonies

Rhode Island

Books in the Thirteen Colonies series include:

The Thirteen Colonies

Rhode Island

Andrew A. Kling

Lucent Books, Inc.
P.O. Box 289011, San Diego, California

On cover: The Landing of Roger Williams by Alonzo Chappell

Library of Congress Cataloging-in-Publication Data

Kling , Andrew A., 1961–
    Rhode Island / by Andrew A. Kling.
        p. cm. — (The thirteen colonies)
Includes bibliographical references (p.) and index.
    Summary: Discusses Rhode Island's beginnings, daily life in the
growing colony, Rhode Island and the American Revolution, and the
colony's decision to ratify the Constitution.
    ISBN 1-56006-873-6 (hardback : alk. paper)
    1. Rhode Island—History—Colonial period, ca. 1600–1775—
Juvenile literature. 2. Rhode Island—History—1775–1865—Juvenile
literature. [1. Rhode Island—History—Colonial period, ca. 1600–1775.
2. Rhode Island—History—1775–1865.] I. Title. II. Thirteen colonies
(Lucent Books)
F82 .K58 2002
974.5'02—dc21

2001000857

Printed in the U.S.A.

Contents

Foreword

T he story of the thirteen English colonies that became the
United States of America is one of startling diversity, conflict,
and cultural evolution. Today, it is easy to assume that the
colonists were of one mind when fighting for independence from
England and afterwards when the national government was created.
However, the American colonies had to overcome a vast reservoir of
distrust rooted in the broad geographical, economic, and social
differences that separated them. Even the size of the colonies
contributed to the conflict; the smaller states feared domination by
the larger ones.

These sectional differences stemmed from the colonies' earliest days.
The northern colonies were more populous and their economies were
more diverse, being based on both agriculture and manufacturing. The
southern colonies, however, were dependent on agriculture—in most
cases, the export of only one or two staple crops. These economic
differences led to disagreements over things such as the trade embargo
the Continental Congress imposed against England during the war.
The southern colonies wanted their staple crops to be exempt from the
embargo because their economies would have collapsed if they could
not trade with England, which in some cases was the sole importer. A
compromise was eventually made and the southern colonies were
allowed to keep trading some exports.

In addition to clashing over economic issues, often the colonies
did not see eye to eye on basic political philosophy. For example,
Connecticut leaders held that education was the route to greater
political liberty, believing that knowledgeable citizens would not
allow themselves to be stripped of basic freedoms and rights.
South Carolinians, on the other hand, thought that the protection
of personal property and economic independence was the basic

foundation of freedom. In light of such profound differences it is amazing that the colonies were able to unite in the fight for independence and then later under a strong national government.

Why, then, did the colonies unite? When the Revolutionary War began the colonies set aside their differences and banded together because they shared a common goal—gaining political freedom from what they considered a tyrannical monarchy—that could be more easily attained if they cooperated with each other. However, after the war ended, the states abandoned unity and once again pursued sectional interests, functioning as little nations in a weak confederacy. The congress of this confederacy, which was bound by the Articles of Confederation, had virtually no authority over the individual states. Much bickering ensued—the individual states refused to pay their war debts to the national government, the nation was sinking further into an economic depression, and there was nothing the national government could do. Political leaders realized that the nation was in jeopardy of falling apart. They were also aware that European nations such as England, France, and Spain were all watching the new country, ready to conquer it at the first opportunity. Thus the states came together at the Constitutional Convention in order to create a system of government that would be both strong enough to protect them from invasion and yet nonthreatening to state interests and individual liberties.

The Thirteen Colonies series affords the reader a thorough understanding of how the development of the individual colonies helped create the United States. The series examines the early history of each colony's geographical region, the founding and first years of each colony, daily life in the colonies, and each colony's role in the American Revolution. Emphasis is given to the political, economic, and social uniqueness of each colony. Both primary and secondary quotes enliven the text, and sidebars highlight personalities, legends, and personal stories. Each volume ends with a chapter on how the colony dealt with changes after the war and its role in developing the U.S. Constitution and the new nation. Together, the books in this series convey a remarkable story—how thirteen fiercely independent colonies came together in an unprecedented political experiment that not only succeeded, but endures to this day.

Introduction

Before the Colony

High atop the dome of the capitol building in Providence, Rhode Island, stands a statue of a man with a spear in one hand and an anchor at his side. The "Independent Man," as he is called, embodies the spirit and history of Rhode Island: a colony that was founded in the spirit of independence of thought and religion and fought to achieve political independence. The anchor symbolizes not only the role that sea trade played in the colony's growth but also the role that faith played in giving the colonists hope for a better future. Indeed, "Hope" remains the state motto today.

"The State of Rhode Island and Providence Plantations," its official name, has its colonial roots in a desire for political and religious freedom. These goals were even loftier than those desired by some of the most ardent English colonists. The Rhode Island colony was not the result of British desires for empire, as were the colonies of North Carolina and Virginia. Rhode Island was not purchased from another European nation, as was the colony of Delaware, nor was it taken from another European nation through force, as was the colony of New York.

Instead, Rhode Island grew out of the desire of a number of men and women who wished to pursue their ideals. These ideals were later embodied in the Declaration of Independence—"all men are created equal"—and in the Bill of Rights—the government "shall make no law respecting an establishment of religion, or prohibiting the free exercise thereof." In fact, more than one hundred years before these famous documents were written, the charter of the Rhode Island colony expressed similar sentiments:

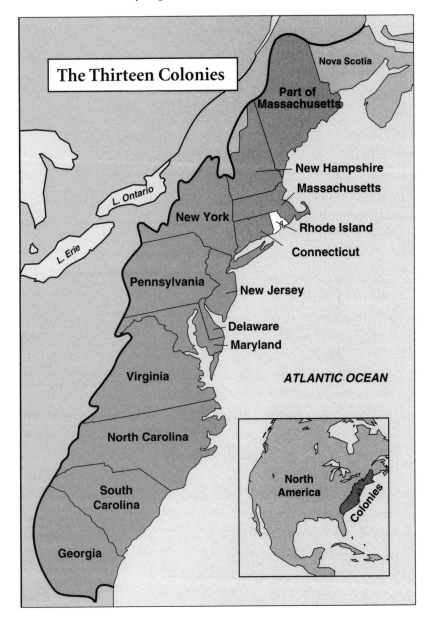

The Thirteen Colonies

Nova Scotia

Part of Massachusetts

New Hampshire

Massachusetts

L. Ontario

New York

Rhode Island

L. Erie

Connecticut

Pennsylvania

New Jersey

Delaware

Maryland

Virginia

ATLANTIC OCEAN

North Carolina

South Carolina

North America

Colonies

Georgia

No person within the sayd colonye, at any tyme hereafter, shall be any wise molested, punished, disquieted, or called in question for any differences in opinion in matters of religion … but that all and every person and persons may, from time to time, and at all times hereafter, freelye and fullye have and enjoy his and theire own judgements and consciences, in matters of religious concernments.[1]

Rhode Island was often at odds with the other colonies because of this charter. Some who lived outside the colony referred to it as "Rogue's Island," convinced that the only people who lived there were religious zealots, scoundrels, ne'er-do-wells, and merchants bent on making money at everyone else's expense. But the lofty words of the 1663 charter captured the intentions of Rhode Island's founders, and helped foster a spirit of independence that became the hallmark of the colony, and of the new state, in a newly independent nation.

Chapter One

Beginnings

In the year 1524, several European nations were participating in the exploration of the New World. Mariners willing to make the perilous journey across the "Western Sea" (today's Atlantic Ocean) were able to sell their services to the highest bidder. Into this scene came Giovanni da Verrazano, hired by France's King Francis I. The king directed Verrazano to sail along the coast of the new continent and explore any substantial waterway in order to find the legendary Northwest Passage to China.

At the time, Spain and Portugal controlled the trade routes around the southern tip of Africa to China and other Asian lands, where treasures such as gold and spices were available for trade. European geographers theorized that a similar route might exist to the west, around or through North America. Discovering this Northwest Passage remained a goal until the explorations of Meriwether Lewis and William Clark, almost three centuries later, finally proved that there was no such water route. But in Verrazano's day, most Europeans believed that the passage existed and that it was only a matter of time before it would be found.

Verrazano's voyage to the Americas resulted in several discoveries for curious geographers. He described the treacherous, shifting shoals along what is today the coast of southern North Carolina; later known as Cape Fear, it first appeared on European maps as "Promontorium Tremendium," the "horrible headland." Verrazano then sailed into the mouth of a river that would later bear the name

Hired to find the Northwest Passage to China, Giovanni da Verrazano sailed to the Americas and discovered Narragansett Bay.

of another explorer, Henry Hudson; today, a narrow part of that river and a suspension bridge across it carry Verrazano's name. He also sailed around a triangular island several miles offshore that reminded him of the Greek isle of Rhodes, then voyaged into a broad bay with several large islands. He met the inhabitants who lived there and described a land covered with oak and walnut trees and filled with game such as deer and lynx. The natives guided him to a sheltered anchorage off a large island they called Aquidneck. In his report to King Francis, Verrazano described them as the "goodliest people and of the fairest conditions that we have found in this our voyage."[2] But after two weeks of their hospitality, and the exploration of this broad bay, Verrazano concluded that this was not the Northwest Passage. In early May, he departed to continue his voyage up the coast.

France failed to follow up on Verrazano's discoveries, and Europeans did not return to the area, later named Narragansett Bay, for ninety years. In 1614, Dutch explorer Adriaen Block visited the coast and described an island of red earth that he called "Roodt Eylandt." Perhaps the modern name *Rhode Island* comes from Block's observations or from Verrazano's writings. Whatever the origins, the next Europeans to have an impact on the areas surrounding Narragansett Bay were not explorers but refugees from already established English colonies to the north and east.

The First Rhode Islanders

Before the arrival of the Europeans, the Narragansett Bay area was home to Native Americans: the Wampanoag on the east side of the bay and the Narragansett on the west. Despite the European explorations and the establishment of English colonies at Plymouth and Massachusetts Bay, these eastern woodland Indians continued to live their lives much as they had for centuries, at least for a while longer.

Scientists today identify the Wampanoag and Narragansett as members of the Algonquin group. Unlike many other Indians, these natives were not nomadic; they had definite areas where they grew crops, caught fish, built homes, held ceremonies, and raised families. Some areas were occupied only during the summer, when the fish were running and the sea breezes made the warm days and nights more comfortable.

Villages were usually located by a river or an area of coastline that allowed easy access to fishing grounds; many were established on bluffs that had a view of the surrounding area. Some settlements were surrounded by a stockade to protect them from animals or rival tribes. The Narragansett and Wampanoag grew various crops in the villages, including corn, beans, squash, and pumpkins. The nearby woods were a source of game animals such as turkey, deer, and moose, and plant foods such as wild berries, mushrooms, and nuts from hickory and elm trees. The waters provided not only clams, lobsters, and various types of fish, but perhaps even the occasional whale, found beached along the shore.

Family life within the Narragansett and Wampanoag settlements revolved around their homes, or wigwams. The wigwam consisted of a frame of thin green saplings bent in a half-circle and then planted in the ground. More saplings were bent around this frame and lashed to it to form a circular, dome-shaped structure. A covering of elm bark was then tied to the frame, leaving a smoke hole in the top and a doorway at the bottom. Occasionally, animal skins or dried grass was added to the covering for additional protection, and sometimes pieces of sod were used for insulation against winter winds.

The wigwam was usually small, designed for individual families. The cozy interior had a fire pit in the center and shelves and benches around the outside walls. The family slept on the ground, on mats or fur robes, with their feet toward the fire.

The Narragansett and Wampanoag had many traditional customs. One of the customs that puzzled Europeans was gift giving.

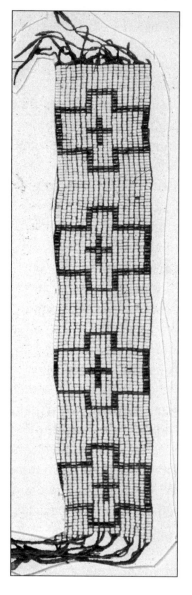

Wampum belts, highly prized and made from seashells, were used as ceremonial jewelry and as money.

The process of giving gifts was dictated by the occasion and by a person's social stature. For example, it was expected for the family of a young man about to get married to give gifts to the family of the bride, and vice versa. According to another tradition, a man who had killed another had to give gifts to the deceased's family in order to save his own life.

The man who gave generously was highly respected among his people. Traditionally, gifts had been items such as tobacco, beaver pelts, animal skins, barks, and ointments. With the arrival of the new settlers, however, other gifts such as colored blankets, lace, and manufactured metal objects like pots and scissors became available and highly sought after.

The most prized gift of all was wampum, shell beads strung together into various forms. Before the introduction of European tools, wampum was very difficult to make. White wampum was made from the inside of conch shells, and the more valuable dark blue or purple wampum was made from the shells of mussels or quahog clams. Wampum beads, rarely more than half an inch long, first had to be cut out of the shells with stone tools. Next, a small hole was bored from end to end, through which a narrow strip of deerskin was inserted to make necklaces, bracelets, or belts.

Presents of wampum were often given at diplomatic councils among tribes. The greater the gift, the greater the respect accorded to the giver. Although wampum was not money in the modern sense, one historian describes its uses "as ceremonial jewelry . . . in rituals of tribute and consolation by Indian leaders, and sometimes . . . in exchange for other items."[3]

Native Leadership

The Narragansett and Wampanoag were led by a primary chief called a sachem. The sachems were often the sons of earlier leaders, inheriting the title when their fathers died. Sometimes they were appointed as sachem because of an act of bravery in war. The sachems were different from the leaders to which the European explorers and settlers were accustomed.

Sachems were not like the kings and queens of Europe, who ruled with absolute power. According to historian Patrick Malone, "English observers had great difficulty in comprehending the limits of [the sachems'] authority."[4] They also were not like the ministers and priests of Western society, whose religious dictates often carried as much weight as those of the monarchs. The sachems' roles were most often advisory, suggesting courses of action for their followers. It was not unusual for the English to talk with a sachem and then assume that the decisions reached in those discussions were binding policy for all Indians and Europeans. In reality, however, the sachem would communicate the decisions to his people, but individuals or groups who disagreed were free to follow their own course of action.

This was the natives' own form of democracy. Each individual was responsible for his or her own actions and was able to follow his or her own conscience and express a particular opinion. Such individuality led to fluid politics, ever-changing alliances, and eventual conflict with neighbors—both Indian and European.

The Narragansett and the Wampanoag were at various times allies and enemies, depending on leadership and current events. With the advent of the English, both groups became caught up in the political intrigues of the newcomers. They were subject to shifting alliances with the varying colonies during the colonists' territorial and religious conflicts.

The relations between the first Rhode Islanders and the newcomers were cordial for many years. But it is unlikely that the land's original inhabitants were able to anticipate that an Englishman's desire for freedom of expression would lead to great changes around Narragansett Bay.

Roger Williams

Little is known about the early life of that Englishman, Roger Williams. Historians agree that he was born in England around 1603. He and his wife left England in 1631 for the fledgling English colony in Massachusetts Bay in order to pursue Williams's dream of religious freedom.

Williams had been somewhat of a thorn in the side of England's official church, the Anglican Church. He dared to question established church practices concerning religious services and the church's role in the lives of its members. An invitation to preach from the church in the village of Salem in the Massachusetts Bay Colony seemed to offer a way to escape harassment in England.

But almost as soon as he arrived in Massachusetts, he drew the attention of the colony's Puritan leadership. Williams had some very definite views on the state of affairs in the New World and on the way the colony was run. He felt that there should be a true separation between the church and the civil leadership. In the Massachusetts colony, the government and the Puritan Church worked hand in hand to run the settlements. Elected officials were often church leaders as well. So, through these government positions, church officials dictated laws and social customs. Anyone could be arrested, fined, and punished physically for real or imagined breaches of the Sabbath, which lasted from sundown Saturday to sundown Sunday. These punishments were imposed not by the church officials but by civil authorities. Williams's views, therefore,

Roger Williams

Roger Williams is today best known as the founder of Providence and the colony of Rhode Island. But there was much more to this complex individual. His political, philosophical, and religious contributions live on more than three centuries later.

Roger Williams was fascinated by the Indians' culture and language. In fact, he was one of the few Englishmen who took the time to learn the native Algonquin language. He eventually compiled a dictionary of the local language for the English-speaking colonists, and his 1643 *Key into the Language of America* is considered one of the first American works of anthropology and linguistics.

Williams was also fascinated with the study of God. His own religious beliefs evolved over the years. He challenged the mainstream Puritan beliefs surrounding worship and salvation and began to feel that infant baptism was not sufficient for salvation. He began to preach that adult baptism was an important feature of faith. Williams and those who followed this belief founded America's first Baptist congregation in 1639. However, just four months later, he left the church. Thereafter, until his death, he preferred to call himself a "Seeker," or someone who was dissatisfied with the regular organization of any particular church and who sought instead the good elements to be found in all forms of worship.

Roger Williams died in 1683. At his request, he was buried in an unmarked grave in the original town site of Providence. Later, bones that were purported to be his were relocated and reburied along the heights of the east side of the city in Prospect Park. Today, a heroic granite statue of Williams stands at the edge of the cliff, looking out over the city he founded.

Roger Williams

were inflammatory. He felt that the magistrates should have no say over religious matters. He wrote, "Forced worship stinks in God's nostrils."[5]

Since he had worn out his welcome in the Boston area, Williams traveled south to the nearby Plymouth Colony. The Pilgrims who administered Plymouth Colony were generally more tolerant of opinions that differed from established doctrine than their Puritan brethren to the north. Williams was invited to preach, yet after a time his views became difficult for his new neighbors to swallow. When he started preaching that the king of England had no right to make grants of land to the colonies because the land belonged to the original inhabitants, the American Indians, the Massachusetts officials had heard enough and found him guilty of spreading "newe & dangerous opinions against the authoritie of magistrates."[6] They ordered that Williams be arrested and deported to England.

Fortunately for Williams, he still had a few friends who looked out for him, and one told him of the arrest order. Williams and a handful of others fled from the Plymouth Colony in the winter of 1636, traveling southwest into the snowy wilderness. They eventually reached the shores of what is today the Seekonk River in the domain of the Wampanoag Indians. Williams had spent time among the Wampanoag before and had become friends with their chief, Ousamequin (also known as Massasoit), whose winter headquarters were in the area. The natives assisted Williams and his friends by giving them food and shelter. In the spring, the English built houses and sowed crops, but they soon received word that they were still within the borders of the Plymouth Colony. They would have to leave the area or risk the still-standing threat of deportation.

Williams crossed the Seekonk estuary into the territory of the Narragansett Indians, the same Indians who had shown Verrazano such hospitality over a hundred years earlier. Legend has it that when Williams came ashore, he was met by several Narragansett with the greeting "What cheer, Netop!"[7] which is translated as "What news, friend!"

Narragansett Indians guide Roger Williams to the future site of Providence, Rhode Island.

The Narragansett knew Williams to be an Englishman of good character, and they viewed him as fair and honest. (Even Williams's detractors among the colonists viewed him as a kind and gentle man who had considerable charm. It was his religious opinions that they couldn't stand.) When Williams explained that he wished to start a settlement beyond the borders of the Plymouth Colony, the Indians took him north to an area just below the place where the Moshassuck River flowed into the Woonasquatucket River. Here, near the head of Narragansett Bay, a natural spring bubbled out of the ground on a plain at the base of a wooded bluff.

With fresh water, access to fishing, nearby flatlands for growing food, and woodlands for building materials, Williams felt that he

The Narragansett Indians greet Williams and his fellow refugees. The Narragansett agreed to let them settle near the head of Narragansett Bay.

could not find a more ideal location for a settlement. He negotiated with Ousamequin and two Narragansett leaders, Canonicus and Miantonomo, who agreed to let the refugees settle there. Williams was nothing if not a man of conviction, and he would not have settled there if the native leaders had disagreed. He later wrote,

> I, having made covenantes of peaceable neighborhood with all the sachems and natives about us, and having in a sense of God's merciful providence unto me in my distresse, called the place Providence; I desired it might be for a shelter for persons distressed of conscience.[8]

The name remains to this day.

The Search for Religious Freedom

Williams hoped to establish a settlement where people could speak their minds freely, without fear of intolerance or religious persecution. In time, many others whose religious beliefs were outside of the mainstream of Puritan or Pilgrim America joined Williams in his colony, which became known as Providence Plantations.

Another settlement, led by Anne Hutchinson, was established on Aquidneck Island, in the southern part of the bay. Like Williams, Hutchinson was a refugee from Massachusetts who had been banished from the colony. Williams spoke with Canonicus and Miantonomo and arranged for the new arrivals to settle on Aquidneck Island. Other religious dissenters, including John Clarke and William Coddington, joined Hutchinson and her husband, William, when they left Massachusetts. They established the community of Pocasset in 1638 (which was renamed Portsmouth in 1643). Coddington and other members of that community split off from the main body the next year, moving south on the island to a fine harbor that Verrazano had explored. Here, they established a settlement called Newport.

William Coddington and other members of the Pocasset community moved to a harbor and founded the town of Newport (pictured).

Anne Hutchinson

Anne Hutchinson's fortune, or perhaps her misfortune, was to be ahead of her time. Her contributions to history far exceed the role she played in the founding of Pocasset (present-day Portsmouth, Rhode Island) and her views on religious freedom. She was an outspoken woman who advocated women's rights, free speech, and the separation of church and state.

Anne Marbury was born in 1591 to a clergyman father and education-minded mother, and married William Hutchinson, a prosperous merchant, in 1612. After settling in Boston in 1634, Hutchinson established Monday meetings for the community's women, during which she repeated Sunday's sermon. Eventually, she began to interpret the lessons in her own ways. Many of the women were attracted to her idea that salvation was obtained through God's love, not only through obedience to church doctrine.

This was tantamount to heresy for the Puritan leadership. In 1637, Hutchinson was brought to trial for holding meetings dishonorable to the church. She might have been let off with a warning had she not spoken at length toward the end of the trial, expressing her views on personal divine revelation. She was sentenced to house arrest until the spring, to be followed by banishment from the colony.

Samuel Gorton established a fourth settlement on the west side of Narragansett Bay, south of Providence. Gorton was known as the "firebrand of New England" because of his religious pronouncements: He felt that any believer in God was qualified to preach, including women; he refused to accept Anglican Church sacraments such as baptism and communion; and he was an ardent advocate of religious freedom and the separation of church and state. He had left the Massachusetts Bay Colony and then the Plymouth Colony because of arguments with the church leadership and the courts. When his opinions about civil and religious authority led to clashes with the religious and political leaders of both Providence and Portsmouth, Gorton and his followers purchased an enormous tract of land from the Narragansett. Here, they established a settlement called Warwick.

Before Hutchinson left Boston to join her husband, who had gone ahead to Rhode Island to set up their new home, she issued a final blast to the Puritan leadership, saying that God does not judge as man does. According to author Elizabeth Anticaglia, in *Twelve American Women*, Hutchinson proclaimed, "Better to be cast out of the church than to deny Christ."

Anne Hutchinson stands trial before the General Court in 1637.

As these settlements grew, they earned a reputation as havens for those persecuted for their religious beliefs. One group for whom the shores of Narragansett Bay offered safe refuge was the Society of Friends, also known as Quakers. The Friends' religious views and pacifism led them to refuse to take oaths of allegiance to either the king of England or the Puritan Church. Furthermore, they refused to take part in the periodic skirmishes with the Indians, a refusal that colonial leadership viewed as a threat to the whole community. In 1656, Massachusetts passed the first of a series of laws that inflicted harsh punishments on Quakers and Quaker sympathizers. According to one historian, the punishments included "imprisonment, fines, and banishment [and later included] whipping, branding, ear-cropping and tongue-boring."[9] As a result, many Quakers in the Massachusetts and Connecticut colonies were

The first Society of Friends meetinghouse was established in 1699 in Newport. The Friends, also called Quakers, came to Newport to escape religious persecution.

forced to find homes elsewhere. In 1657, a group of Quakers arrived in Newport, and members of this group established the nation's first Friends meetinghouse in 1699.

The Quakers were not the only ones to make new homes in the four Narragansett Bay settlements. Newport became home to a group of Jewish refugees from the Caribbean, Spanish, and Portuguese families attracted by the promise of religious freedom. Soon after their arrival in 1658, they formed a congregation, and in 1763 they dedicated Touro Synagogue, North America's oldest synagogue. French Huguenots (who were discriminated against in Catholic France because of their Protestant beliefs) arrived in 1686 and settled on the west side of Narragansett Bay in the town of East Greenwich.

These new settlements continued to grow slowly over the next several years. The officials in neighboring Massachusetts and Connecticut were wary of this growth. They felt threatened by the influx of settlers who did not conform to their religious views.

Some officials tried to control the Narragansett Bay communities by petitioning the English courts to expand the borders of the established colonies to include the Narragansett Bay area, thus making individuals such as Roger Williams and Samuel Gorton subject to established church doctrine and civil laws. Faced with these threats, Williams and others who felt as he did decided it was time to act to protect their interests and their freedoms.

Chapter Two

A "Lively Experiment"

It seemed only logical to Roger Williams and other community leaders that the four original settlements surrounding Narragansett Bay—Providence, Newport, Warwick, and Portsmouth—should be recognized by the English crown as independent from their colonial neighbors. However, the Massachusetts colonies to the east and north, and the Connecticut colonies to the west, refused to acknowledge the Narragansett Bay settlements as self-determining entities. They continued to claim land surrounding the bay that adjoined their colonial borders. Williams and the other leaders of the Narragansett Bay settlements felt that there should be no question that their English outposts were separate and independent from the others.

The Colony's First Charter

It was in this frame of mind that Williams journeyed to London in 1643. He wrote that, "Upon the frequent exception taken by Massachusetts that we had no authority for civil government, I went purposely to England"[10] to obtain a charter that would officially unite the four communities into one colony. A charter was a document, issued by the king of England, that granted land to an individual or groups of individuals who wished to establish new settlements in territories claimed by the English. The charter Williams received in 1644 assured that religious and political freedom would be maintained in the colony, which was called the "Providence Plantations in Narragansett Bay." When Williams returned to the New World, he worked to unite Providence, Warwick, Newport, and Portsmouth under this charter. After several concerns over the formation of a colony government and religious toleration were settled through negotiations, all the settlements recognized the charter in 1647.

The 1644 charter did little to clarify the issue of borders beyond stating that the new colony was granted the lands they had purchased from the Indians and the areas bordering the colonies of Massachusetts, Plymouth, and Connecticut. But it did guarantee the spirit of political and religious independence that Williams sought. It was also based on Williams's beliefs that a civil government was only as powerful as the people who established it and could only exist with the people's consent. However, Williams's views of free government had limits; not everyone who came to the Narragansett Bay colonies was automatically eligible to vote. The new arrival first had to be granted land, and then the right to vote, by the community's town meeting. The right to vote also applied only to male landowners. Nevertheless, Williams's view that citizens should have the right to change their own government was novel and daring for the time.

Other people within the Narragansett Bay settlements, however, sought a different fate for the new colony. William Coddington, one of the founders of Newport, was hoping that the Aquidneck Island villages would become allied with the newly formed New England Confederation (the Massachusetts, Plymouth, Connecticut, and New Haven colonies) or at least with the Massachusetts Bay or Plymouth Colony. When Williams returned from London to establish the colony's new government, Coddington tried to hinder his efforts. He even traveled to London himself to argue for a separate charter for the Aquidneck settlements. He hoped that he would be named governor of Aquidneck Island (which the settlers had renamed Rhode Island in the spirit of Verrazano's visit) and neighboring Conanicut Island. Coddington's wish was granted in 1651 when a charter declared him governor for life over these islands.

Not surprisingly, this appointment rankled Williams, the colony's governor. In December 1651, he and John Clarke traveled to England to argue that Coddington's charter should be revoked. At a time when an Atlantic crossing was arduous at best, a winter voyage was something undertaken only by the truly brave of heart. Their efforts were rewarded when the English Council of State revoked Coddington's appointment.

A New Charter

These disputes over charters reflect the political turmoil in England at the time. The English Parliament had deposed King Charles I in 1642 and ruled the nation for the next eighteen years. The monarchy was restored in 1660 when the son of Charles I became king. Charles II annulled all the actions taken by Parliament after it had deposed his father, actions that included Roger Williams's 1644 charter. The charter's legality was now in doubt, and the Narragansett Bay settlers were greatly concerned that the new king might revoke it in part or entirely.

The colony's government authorized John Clarke, who had remained in England since his winter voyage with Roger Williams in 1651, to lobby the king for royal recognition of the Narragansett Bay settlements. Clarke's petition to the king declared that the people of Narragansett Bay "have it much in

Britain's King Charles II (pictured) annulled Roger Williams's 1644 colonial charter.

their hearts, if they may be permitted, to hold forth a lively experiment, that a flourishing and civil state may stand, yea and best be maintained, and that among English spirits, with a full liberty in religious commitments."[11] Charles II was a firm believer in an established church, religious conformity, and the divine right of kings. But in 1663 he granted the Providence plantations a new charter, which in the spirit of Clarke's words included the distinctive phrase a "lively experiment."

The 1663 Charter of Rhode Island and Providence Plantations gave Rhode Island its lengthy title that remains the state's official name today. It also clarified the colony's borders, putting an end to other colonies' claims for the heart of Rhode Island's lands. More important, it reaffirmed the colony's reason for being. It stated that Rhode Island was to be a "lively experiment" in religious freedom, and it gave the colony broad rights of self-government, which was unheard-of in an era of religious intolerance and the absolute rule of kings. Rhode Island was not subject to a royal governor who was appointed from England; it was free to elect its own governor and government officials. This experiment became the first true democracy in the New World, and it blazed a path for the creation of the United States's own innovative political system.

Receiving the new charter reinvigorated the Rhode Islanders' sense of purpose. Over time, the charter itself became a revered artifact at the center of government ceremonies. During each gubernatorial inauguration, the charter was turned over from the old governor to the new for safekeeping. The box in which the charter had been sent from England still held the original document; during the ceremony, the box was opened and the charter taken out for the assembled citizens to observe. The charter was then read aloud, word by word. The leaders felt that the original words of the charter were more effective at reminding the citizens of Rhode Island's special nature than any rhetoric they could provide would be. The citizens of Rhode Island might not have been able to agree on the best way to worship, but with this charter, they could agree on the best way to unite their community, through the worship of political freedom.

The 1663 Royal Charter

The following excerpts from the 1663 charter highlight some of the special rights and privileges granted to the colony of Rhode Island and Providence Plantations. The full text of the charter can be found on the website of Yale University's Avalon Project.

> That our royall will and pleasure is, that noe person within the sayd colonye, at any tyme hereafter, shall bee any wise molested, punished, disquieted, or called in question, for any differences in opinione in matters of religion, and doe not actually disturb the civill peace of our sayd colony; but that all ... freelye and fullye have and enjoye his and theire owne judgments and consciences, in matters of religious concernments. ...

> [A]nd from tyme to tyme, to make, ordeyne, constitute or repeal, such lawes statutes, orders and ordinances ... and magistracye as to them shall seeme meete for the good and wellfare of the sayd Company. ...

> [T]hat yearelie ... the Governour, Deputy-Governour and Assistants of the sayd Company ... to proceede to a new election of one or more of their Company ... and immediately upon and after such elections or elections made, ... the authoritie, office and power, before given to the former Governour, Deputy-Governour, and other officer and officers, soe removed.

The charter of 1663 was good news for those who saw the Rhode Island colony as a haven for persons who wished to follow their own religious consciences. But even though this charter was a turning point for the colony, one of even greater significance occurred just a few years later with the outbreak of war with the Native Americans. The war presented a challenge to the survival of the colony's experiment, as well as the survival of the colonists themselves.

Natives and Settlers Clash

By 1675, there were about 4,000 Europeans living in the colony of Rhode Island. At the same time, there were roughly 5,000 living in the neighboring Plymouth Colony and 17,000 in the Massachusetts Bay Colony. These newcomers were sharing the landscape with approximately 5,000 Narragansett and 2,500 Nipmuck and Mohegan Indians in Rhode Island and southeastern Connecticut, and just over 1,000 Wampanoag on the eastern shores of Narragansett Bay.

The Wampanoag were led by one of Ousamequin's sons, Metacomet. Metacomet's brother Wamsutta had become the leader of the Wampanoag when Ousamequin died; Metacomet succeeded his brother in 1662 when Wamsutta died under mysterious circumstances. Metacomet is better known to history as King Philip, because the English habitually named Indian leaders after European kings and queens. (This practice allowed the English to

Pictured is an Indian family of the Narragansett Bay area. Initially, relations between the Indians and English colonists were friendly.

use their own language to identify individuals whose language they did not understand.)

Metacomet continued the friendly relations with the English established by his father, and he was fond of English fashion and English tools and firearms. However, he had nagging suspicions that the English had poisoned Wamsutta following his brother's visit to Duxbury in the Massachusetts Bay Colony. He also objected to the fact that the Wampanoag and other Indians were being brought before the English courts for violations of English law and punished. Metacomet felt that the Wampanoag were being treated as a subject race even though they had not been defeated in battle.

In February 1675, an Indian named John Sassamon was found dead beneath the ice of a pond in the Plymouth Colony. Sassamon was one of many so-called Praying Indians who had converted to Christianity through the teachings of Englishmen such as the Reverend John Eliot. Sassamon had helped Eliot translate the Bible into his native language, and later served as a translator and secretary to Metacomet. When colonial officials examined his body, they found that his neck had been broken. The English authorities concluded that Sassamon had been murdered.

During the investigation that followed, Plymouth governor Josiah Winslow revealed that Sassamon had come to see him with disturbing news. According to Winslow, Sassamon claimed that Metacomet was attempting to unite the Indian tribes in order to drive out the English. Winslow had informed the Plymouth magistrates, who had in turn conferred with authorities in Massachusetts Bay's capital, Boston. The English officials surmised that Sassamon's conversation with Winslow had led to his death.

Eventually, another Praying Indian offered information that led to the arrest of three Wampanoag, who were tried for Sassamon's murder. A jury of twelve Englishmen and six Indians found them guilty, and they were executed in June 1675. Perhaps that would have been the end of matters had rumors of Indian preparations for war not persisted. But English settlers in outlying communities reported strange sights in the sky, such as blazing comets in the form of fiery arrows, and the sound of gunfire when no one was present.

Metacomet, known by the colonists as King Philip, objected to Indians being punished for violating English laws.

On June 17, several prominent Rhode Islanders, led by deputy-governor John Easton, met with Metacomet to determine his intentions and to try to dissuade him if he was indeed planning for war. They assured him that the king and Rhode Island would respect the rights of the Indians under the law. Their efforts were unsuccessful, however, for Metacomet's views on English law had been well expressed the year before when he had spoken out on disputes between the English and the Indians. These disputes had always been settled in the newcomers' courts, and whenever damages were assessed, the Indians were forced to pay for all damages in land. Metacomet had said, "Thus tract after tract is gone. But little remains of my ancestors' domain. I am resolved not to live to see the day when I have no country."[12] Just three days after Easton's meeting with Metacomet, what has become known as King Philip's War began.

King Philip's War

On Sunday, June 20, 1675, several Wampanoag rampaged through Swansea in the Plymouth Colony. Many Swansea residents had fled their homes for the safety of the village center because rumors of Indian attacks had grown over the preceding few days. The Wampanoag who came to Swansea that day at first ransacked property and harassed several colonists but injured no one. One account claims that the killing began when the pillagers entered a house they thought was deserted. They surprised a man and his son inside; the two had fled from the house under the threat of war and then returned to check on it. When the Wampanoag startled the man and his son, the youngster fired his musket and mortally wounded one of the Indians.

According to one historian, Metacomet had been told by his medicine men that he could win only if the English started the fighting. Since his warriors had provoked the enemy into doing this, it seemed an auspicious beginning for the Indians. Metacomet's people saw the death of the Wampanoag outside of Swansea as an omen for their success and an invitation for an all-out war with the English.

Not all the Indians in the area felt the same way. The Narragansett, Metacomet's neighbors across the bay, at first wished to stay neutral in the growing conflict, but Massachusetts officials meeting with Narragansett representatives in Wickford, Rhode Island, in July made demands the Narragansett found distasteful. They were told that they should treat the Wampanoag as their enemies and that any Wampanoag they found should be turned over to the English. Canonchet, the son of Miantonomo, who led the Narragansett, felt that he must side with the Wampanoag. Canonchet believed that, even if the Narragansett complied with their demands, the Massachusetts leaders would find some excuse to assert force in order to obtain the remaining Narragansett lands.

Canonchet, leader of the Narragansett, sided with the Wampanoag in King Philip's War because he did not want to comply with the white colonists' demands.

When the Narragansett allied with the Wampanoag, the war threatened to involve the English settlers in Rhode Island. The conflict was not a war of Rhode Island's making. The colony officials thought they could remain neutral, but in fact their practices were not entirely neutral. They allowed Massachusetts and Plymouth armies to march across Rhode Island, and in the coming conflict, all of English Rhode Island's mainland settlements were destroyed.

The War in Rhode Island

The first major battle of the war, known as the Great Swamp Fight, took place on December 19, 1675, in southwestern Rhode Island in the Narragansett winter homelands. An Indian defector led an army of eleven hundred from Massachusetts, Plymouth, and Connecticut through a secret path in the woods to an undefended area of the encampment. When the battle began, someone set fire to a wigwam, and a heavy winter wind whipped the fire through the camp, burning to death hundreds, including women, children, and the aged in addition to the fighting men. The Indians were routed, and the English killed as many people who fled the scene as they could.

Canonchet and many of his warriors escaped the carnage at the Great Swamp. He joined his forces with Metacomet, and over the next six months waged war upon the English, reaching as far north as Boston. On March 26, 1676, Canonchet and his men surrounded a company of fifty-five Plymouth soldiers near Central Falls, Rhode Island. The soldiers had been sent to capture him; instead, the Indians wiped out the entire force. The next day, they marched on Providence, six miles south of Central Falls.

Roger Williams, one of the founders of Rhode Island, and always a good friend of the Narragansett, was one of a handful of settlers left in the town. Most of the citizens of Providence had been evacuated to the villages on Aquidneck Island. Williams, now more than seventy years old, tried to convince the Narragansett that further bloodshed was unnecessary. The Narragansett agreed not to harm him and the twenty-seven men with him, saying, "Brother

Roger Williams tried to persuade the Narragansett to end the war. The Indians spared Williams and his company but burned the town of Providence.

Williams, you are a good man; you have been kind to us many years; not a hair of your head shall be touched,"[13] but they did not spare the town. Providence was put to the torch while Williams and the others waited out the flames in the safety of a blockhouse.

Another slaughter of Indian men, women, and children occurred near Warwick in July. The war became a defensive one for the Indians. The Mohawk and other nearby nations declined to join the fight in New England. Connecticut soldiers had captured

Canonchet in April; when they told him he was to be executed, he proclaimed, "I shall die before my heart is soft, or I have said anything unworthy of myself."[14] Metacomet was killed by one of his own people in August. The remaining warriors were hunted down mercilessly and slain wherever they were found. Metacomet's wife, his nine-year-old son, and most of the Narragansett and Wampanoag captives held by the Massachusetts, Plymouth, and Connecticut forces were sold into slavery.

Rhode Island had passed a law in 1674 prohibiting the sale of Indians into slavery, but the settlers felt differently following the

The Narragansett

King Philip's War was a tragic turn of events for the Narragansett, who had previously had generally good relations with the European newcomers. They had welcomed the English and other Europeans as neighbors. King Philip's War quashed those neighborly feelings. The Europeans vanquished the natives and subjected them to imprisonment, slavery, and execution.

The Narragansett who survived the war and escaped Rhode Island traveled great distances to maintain their freedom. Some were granted asylum by the Niantic, their neighbors in Connecticut. Others may have traveled as far away as Wisconsin and Canada and settled down in new homes. The Narragansett living in Rhode Island today are likely a mix of Narragansett, Niantic, Wampanoag, and other American Indian groups who strive to maintain their culture and heritage.

Recently, the Narragansett and Wampanoag petitioned Harvard University for the return of the remains of two dozen bodies in a Harvard museum under the 1990 Native American Graves Protection and Repatriation Act. The act was designed to return remains of Native Americans that have become part of museum collections, and has helped to heal some of the wounds between American Indians and European Americans across the United States. Perhaps the remains at Harvard will one day return to their people.

war. Roger Williams supervised a compromise practice in which the Indians who had surrendered to Rhode Islanders were sold into temporary servitude. An Indian five years old or younger was to be set free at the age of thirty; those over thirty would serve their masters for seven years. Williams headed the committee that divided the profits from the sale of the Indians among the settlers of Providence whose homes had been destroyed. For a man who had hoped that the colonists and the natives could live in peace and brotherhood, the war had been a terrible blow. Williams believed that the Indians had lost their self-respect and dignity over the years

Pictured is a medicine man of the Narragansett Tribe. Today the Narragansett strive to maintain their culture and heritage.

of associating with the English, which resulted in the gradual destruction of their original way of life.

A New Generation

The end of King Philip's War brought to a close a pivotal chapter in Rhode Island's history. The defeat of the Narragansett and the Wampanoag had removed the Indians as a threat to the English settlements. By the end of the war, the men and women who had struggled to obtain religious freedom and whose efforts had resulted in the 1663 charter were beginning to pass from the scene. John Clarke died in 1676; Samuel Gorton in 1677; William Coddington in 1678; and Roger Williams in 1683. These leaders were replaced by a new generation of Rhode Islanders whose religious freedom was an established right. It was up to this new generation to rebuild the colony and to maintain its "lively experiment."

Chapter Three

Daily Life in the Growing Colony

As the eighteenth century began, Rhode Islanders were concentrating on expanding the colony's economy following the devastation that had occurred during King Philip's War. By 1700, some seven thousand Europeans lived in the colony, scattered among the largest towns of Providence and Newport and smaller communities such as Warwick, Charlestown, East Greenwich, and Jamestown. Rhode Islanders developed new settlements to the west and to the north of Narragansett Bay, clearing forests for timber and for farmland. They also started to take advantage of the Bay's bounty of fish and shellfish. All this activity led to Rhode Island's growth in the eighteenth century. More available land and resources brought more settlers to the colony, and more settlers brought an expanding economy through business and trade.

The colony's civic leaders were interested in increasing opportunities for Rhode Island's citizens, and they encouraged opportunities for new business and trade. New opportunities for education, however, were fewer than those available to residents of other colonies. Rhode Islanders who wished to pursue an advanced education were obliged to leave the colony, and sometimes were hindered by what little education they had received in Rhode Island. Historian Samuel Eliot Morison wrote,

> Only one boy from Rhode Island, so far as we know, attended college in the entire seventeenth century. He did not manage to enter [Harvard] until the age of twenty-one, and he was allowed to graduate in three years, on the plea of his age, and his petition to the effect that a great part of his life "hath been Spent in a land of darknesse prophanesse [disrespect for religious beliefs and practices] Sabbath breaking and Atheisme."[15]

Whether these were the words of the student from Block Island or of the Harvard records is unclear. But they serve to point out the lack of educational opportunities in Rhode Island in comparison with some of the other colonies.

Education Often Linked to Religious Doctrine

While other colonies spent time, energy, and money establishing schools and colleges such as Harvard, Yale, Columbia, and William and Mary, efforts to establish public education in Rhode Island were, for the most part, haphazard. Rhode Islanders' lack of interest in such endeavors lay in the very nature of the colony itself. Because of the efforts of early leaders such as Roger Williams, John Clarke, and Anne Hutchinson, and because of the established doctrine of religious tolerance, there was little support for an education that would teach one belief over another. The Puritan leaders who had established Harvard, for example, felt that education was the best way to increase knowledge of the Bible and to ensure humans' salvation. Officers of the Episcopalian Church controlled William and Mary University in Virginia, and the Reformed Dutch Church ran Rutgers College (today Rutgers University) in New Jersey. The various denominations of religious dissenters in Rhode Island saw no need for faith-based education. How one's neighbor believed and practiced religion was his business and his alone. The 1663 charter had proclaimed this, and Rhode Islanders believed in it fervently.

Although faith-based education was not popular in Rhode Island, there were individuals and groups who wished to develop nonreligious schools. From time to time, some citizens tried to establish some form of schooling for the colony's youth, as this announcement taken from records of day-to-day business in Newport suggests:

> Quarter meeting, April 17, 1709.—Mr. William Gilbert being chosen schoolmaster for ye town of Newport, and proposing that upon conditions, the quarter meeting grant him of the benefit of the school land, viz., the chamber and sellar and the profit arising from ye school land in this part of the town and some conveniency for keeping fire in the winter season, he is willing to teach school for the year ensuing, and to begin the second Monday in May next, voated and allowed an act of the quarter meeting.[16]

Many individuals advertised their services as instructors throughout the years, but no school survived for very long in an era without guarantees of financial support from a community or a church. Providence gave a man named George Taylor permission to keep a school in a room in the Colony House in 1735, and around 1750 the town built a regular schoolhouse on Meeting Street. But educational opportunities were often open only to those who could afford the tuition. Furthermore, the ability to read and write was rarely seen as an essential tool for living. A farmer did not need to know how to write to be able to count the number of chickens in his flock or the number of eggs they laid each month. But the main reason the colony's attempts at establishing formal education were tentative at best, and unsuccessful overall, was simply that most of the colony's families had more important things for their children to do.

Brown University

Brown University in Providence was created through the efforts of several individuals who saw the need for an institution of higher learning in Rhode Island. The founding of the college illustrates that some of the colony's citizens were interested in improving Rhode Island's future through new educational opportunities.

As Rhode Island became less isolated and ships began to visit ports throughout the colonies, they began to carry mail among friends, families, and organizations. In the late 1750s, a group of Baptists in Rhode Island were corresponding with their counterparts in Pennsylvania. The Rhode Islanders suggested that the Pennsylvanians help them establish a Baptist college in Rhode Island. James Manning, a Baptist who had recently graduated from Princeton College in New Jersey, arrived in Rhode Island in 1763 to organize such a college. He received considerable support from not only Rhode Island Baptists but members of other denominations as well.

"Rhode Island College" was founded in 1764 and received a charter from the Rhode Island General Assembly, although it received no money from the colonial government. This charter, in keeping with the spirit of Rhode Island's heritage, proclaimed that prospective students need not be Baptists to enroll. Quoted in Walter C. Bronson's *The History of Brown University 1764–1914*, the charter maintained that students "shall never be admitted any Religious Tests but on the Contrary all the Members hereof shall for ever enjoy full free Absolute and uninterrupted Liberty of

The Cycle of Life: Eighteenth-Century Rhode Island

Whether a person lived in Newport or on a family farm in Smithfield in the 1700s, the rising and setting of the sun and the cycles of the seasons governed life in colonial Rhode Island. Every day, regardless of the weather, the family had tasks to perform, and each member, except for the very young, had a job.

A small family farm in Rhode Island needed to be virtually self-sufficient. The family grew its own food, which usually consisted of corn, oats, and rye, and a variety of garden vegetables such as

Conscience." The college graduated its first students in Warren, Rhode Island, in 1769. It relocated to Providence in 1770 on land donated by the Brown family. In recognition, the trustees renamed the college Brown University, and it has remained so ever since.

squash, beans, and pumpkins. The family might have also cultivated an apple tree to provide fresh fruit, and scoured the surrounding woods for native grapes, nuts, and berries. The American Indians had introduced the first settlers to the foods that were native to the New World, and in the 1700s, these foods sometimes made the difference between eating and starving.

Corn proved to be the lifeblood for many settlers just as it had been for the American Indians. Roger Williams contended that "*nassaump*, which the English call Samp, is Indian corne beaten and

A man distributes corn rations to his family. Corn, introduced to the settlers by the American Indians, proved to be the lifeblood of the settlers.

eaten hot or cold with milk or butter and is a diet exceeding[ly] wholesome for English bodies."[17] Dozens of uses for corn that have been handed down from the Indians remain to this day, including succotash, hominy, corn pone, and popcorn. A particular form of fried cornmeal cake, called a Jonnycake, remains a favorite among Rhode Islanders today.

A Variety of Livestock

In addition to corn and other crops, the family might also raise a variety of livestock, such as cattle, sheep, pigs, and poultry. Cows provided milk and cream; cheese was made from the curds of sour milk and could be stored in cellars for many months. An eighteenth-century traveler characterized Rhode Island cheese as equal to "the best Cheshire of England or Rocfort [Roquefort] of France."[18] Tallow, or beef fat, was an essential ingredient in making candles, which were the main source of lighting at the time. Beef as a food source was less important than it is today. Cows and bulls were more necessary as breeding stock for oxen, which were the primary beasts of burden.

Chickens provided meat and eggs, and the family diet was usually supplemented by wild game such as turkeys, geese, doves, and pigeons, as well as fish and shellfish. One New England resident recorded some two hundred species of fish that colonists caught and ate. Lobsters weighing more than fifteen pounds were common, and fried, roasted, or boiled eels were considered a delicacy by some.

Sheep provided not only mutton for the dinner table but also wool for clothing. In the days before the widespread use of cotton (and before the invention of artificial fibers), almost every piece of clothing contained some wool. The wool had to be sheared from the sheep, cleaned, carded, and spun into yarn before it could be knitted or woven into cloth. Native plants and berries were used to dye the wool cloth into different colors, but that was an extra step that was not necessary for making day-to-day work clothes.

Clothing could also be made from flax, an annual plant that could be woven into linen cloth. Linen was extremely sturdy, and homemakers used it for a variety of household items, including undergarments, table coverings, and napkins. Enterprising weavers combined wool and linen fibers into a fabric called linsey-woolsey which was both strong and comfortable and combined the best qualities of each component.

Creating linen fibers from flax was an even greater chore than creating wool fibers from sheep. The desirable fibers in the flax plant lie under a tough bark and around a hard core. To make the flax fibers suitable for spinning, the flax stalks first had to be harvested, rippled, retted, braked, and swingled. Rippling stripped the seed heads from the stalks. Bundles of stalks were then weighted down in a stream, or retted, for five days to make the central core brittle enough to be broken into short pieces. Next, the stalks were braked in a wooden press with teeth that broke the stalks but not the fibers. Finally, the bundles were hung over the end of an upright board and beaten with a long wooden swingling knife with scraping, downward strokes, leaving a collection of fibers ready to be combed and spun. Both braking and swingling were arduous tasks requiring great strength, and were generally seen as men's work. A good worker could swingle forty pounds of flax a day.

Seasonal Chores

Each family tried to raise enough food and animals to feed all its members. Anything extra could be sold in exchange for goods or services; for example, a surplus of eggs could be bartered as payment to the local blacksmith. As the days grew longer with the approaching of spring, the family planted crops and hoped that a late winter freeze would not wipe out their efforts. With the arrival of summer, there were sheep to be sheared, calves to be weaned, crops to be tended, eggs to be collected, and cows to be milked. In autumn, crops had to be harvested, and the family had to prepare for the coming winter. Wood needed to be cut and set aside. Meat needed to be dried or salted to preserve it. Fruits and vegetables were dried in cellars or storehouses to keep them from spoiling; they would be important ingredients in the family's diet during the coming cold months. The settlers preserved a wide variety of fruits and vegetables, including plums, peaches, artichokes, cucumbers, walnuts, quinces, grapes, and berries.

Once winter came, a family might be cut off from their friends and neighbors because of the weather. Running out of food or wood could mean disaster. Thus, the challenge was to spend the warmer months productively enough to be able to survive the long New England winters. Yet even in winter there were still animals to

Blacksmiths forged iron shoes for horses and oxen and made kitchen and garden tools.

care for, and everyday tasks such as knitting and sewing to perform, as well as daily family rituals and worship.

A Constant Struggle

In such a climate, survival was a constant struggle. Many children died very young, sometimes living only a few months, weeks, or days before succumbing to various diseases or exposure to the elements. Illnesses such as smallpox, chicken pox, dysentery, and pneumonia that are easily treatable today could wipe out entire families in the 1700s. The typical diet could also bring about debilitating diseases such as scurvy, from lack of vitamin C, and rickets, a vitamin D deficiency. Scurvy causes anemia and bleeding from the gums, nose, and mouth and can lead to death if untreated. Rickets, a bone disease, can cause permanent malformation of the skeleton.

If a child survived the first few months, chances of living into adulthood increased. Still, it was unusual for these men and women to live to an old age by today's standards. Some, like Roger Williams, lived beyond the age of seventy and were considered true marvels of survival.

City Life

There were few differences in survival patterns between those who lived on Rhode Island's farms and those who lived in its towns. Daily life in the towns was not much different from daily life on the farms. As on the farms, Newport or Providence residents usually had a small garden and raised a few animals for their food. However, they did have a few more options than their country brethren when it came to obtaining commodities such as fresh fish or meat, beer, or goods such as cloth or candles. These items were available from various traders, merchants, and craftspeople who set up shop along the towns' waterfronts or on the main streets.

The one significant difference between town life and farm life was that living in the towns afforded more opportunities for pursuing a trade or business than living on a farm did. Blacksmiths taught young apprentices how to forge iron horseshoes and oxen shoes as well as make kitchen and garden tools. Some women advertised their services as seamstresses or cloth makers. Others hired themselves out to families as household help, such as cooks or nannies.

A youngster growing up in Rhode Island in the middle of the 1700s, however, might have dreamt of something larger than working a small farm on Aquidneck Island or establishing a new plantation in the western part of the colony. In the harbor, ships and boats of all description came and went. Trade through shipping had become the new way to become successful in Rhode Island, and Rhode Islanders were eager to compete with and surpass their wealthier colonial neighbors.

A mailman walks by colonial homes in present-day Newport.

The Colonies' Warehouse

By the 1730s, trade dominated the lives of the colony's citizens. Communities were able to provide for themselves and still have time to raise crops and animals for trade. As trade networks between communities and colonies developed, individuals who weren't directly involved with the shipping business found they

Rhode Island became a major trade center in colonial America. Providence, shown here, was ideally located to serve the markets in which most Rhode Islanders traded.

could have a stake in a ship's fortunes as well. An investment in a ship's voyage was similar to investing in today's stock market. It could bring great financial gains if the ship returned from its voyage with a profitable cargo, such as manufactured goods from England, silks from Europe, or slaves from Africa. Of course, an investment could also be lost if the ship sank or was captured by pirates. But as the century wore on, eventually almost everyone in Rhode Island became somehow involved with trade, either directly or indirectly.

The preparations for a voyage began long before the ship set sail. The ship's owners began by sending out orders to markets in the villages and towns. They gathered goods such as cattle, produce, dairy goods, and timber from the settlers as far north as Worcester, Massachusetts, and across both the eastern and western borders of the colony. Live animals were carted to the harbor, and slaughterhouses near the docks prepared the livestock for the voyage. Since there was no refrigeration or metal containers yet, goods were shipped in barrels. Coopers built the barrels to ship the meat, produce, cheese, and other goods.

All of the ship's cargo had to be recorded and tracked, so the owners hired clerks to organize their paperwork. Goods had to be loaded onto the ships, so they employed stevedores to carry the heavy barrels into the ships' holds. Finally, someone had to sail these ships, so they recruited men (and boys) to hoist and repair the sails, maintain the hemp ropes, and keep watch at all hours and in all types of weather. For many Rhode Islanders, employment on a trade ship was an opportunity for advancement. The road to success lay open for those willing to take a chance and to dream.

The Triangle Trade

The enterprising traders of Rhode Island traveled throughout the colonies, but it was the "triangle trade" that began to dominate attention and promise the greatest potential for profit. A ship loaded with rum from Rhode Island sailed to West Africa to sell the cargo to those willing to sell other Africans as slaves. Now overloaded with as many humans that could be crammed belowdecks, the ship then sailed for the West Indies or South America. There, the slaves were sold for molasses, which was shipped to Rhode Island to be distilled into rum. More molasses meant more rum, which in turn meant more slaves, and so on.

For some merchants, slaves were just another commodity, to be bought or sold like cheese or hogs. One Newport merchant who had made a consistent profit from the trade always gave thanks at the Sunday services following the arrival of a slave ship "that a gracious Providence had been pleased to bring to this land of Freedom another cargo of benighted heathen to enjoy the blessings of a Gospel dispensation."[19] For others, however, conditions on board these ships led to a crisis of conscience. For example, the Brown family of Providence had been involved in various forms of shipping trade since the 1720s, and four brothers—Nicholas, Joseph, John, and Moses—became among the colony's leading merchants and entrepreneurs. John's involvement in the slave trade became a source of great debate with Moses, who had joined the

A trader inspects an African slave. Ships from Rhode Island sailed to Africa to trade rum for slaves.

Society of Friends. Because of his Quaker beliefs, Moses viewed the slave trade as immoral. He eventually freed the few slaves he owned and gradually distanced himself from the family's dealings in the triangle trade.

Trade Flourishes

No matter how objectionable the triangle trade was to men like Moses Brown, it and other forms of trade contributed a great deal to the growing economy of Rhode Island. By the 1770s, daily life for most Rhode Islanders involved the business of trade, either directly or indirectly. Residents of Newport or Providence were directly involved in trade through shipping and selling goods. Residents of more rural areas were more indirectly connected; their farm products were sold to merchants who in turn sold them to shipowners. One historian noted that, at the time, Narragansett Bay merchants "owned 200 vessels engaged in foreign trade and another

300 to 400 used in coastal traffic" with "2,200 seamen employed in operating the fleet. . . . No numbers exist for the hundreds of artisans, dockworkers, warehousemen, wagon masters, bookkeepers and other employees of the merchant countinghouses."[20]

Eighteenth-Century Medicine

With the benefit of modern scientific research and knowledge, treatments prescribed for diseases in the eithteenth century can seem quaint or amusing, or more dangerous than the disease itself. The following, which comes from an unnamed source and is quoted in Alice Morse Earle's Customs and Fashions in New England, *was touted as a cure for rickets.*

The admirable and most famous Snail water.—Take a peck of garden Shel Snails, wash them well in Small Beer, and put them in an oven until they have done making a Noise, then take them out and wipe them well from the green froth that is upon them, and bruise them shells and all in a Stone Mortar, then take a Quart of Earthworms, scowre them with salt, slit them, and wash well with water from their filth, and in a stone Mortar beat them in pieces, then lay in the bottom of your distilled pot Angelica two handfuls, and two handfuls of Celandine upon them, to which put two quarts of Rosemary flowers, Bearsfoot, Agrimony, red Dock roots, Bark of Barberries, Betony and Sorrel of each two handfuls, Rue one handful; then lay the Snails and Worms on top of the hearbs and flowers, then pour on three Gallons of the Strongest Ale, and let stand all night, in the morning put three ounces of Cloves beaten, sixpennyworth of beaten Saffron, and on top of them six ounces of shaved Hartshorne, then set on the Limbeck, and close it with paste and so receive the water by pintes, which will be nine in all, and the first is the strongest, whereof take in the morning two spoonfuls in four spoonfuls of small Beer, the like in the afternoon.

Rhode Island's economy had grown to include goods such as horses, cattle, tobacco, flour, timber, and iron goods, which were shipped throughout the colonies and overseas. The colony's merchants were well known in ports of call in the Caribbean, West Africa, and Europe. Enterprising men in Newport and Providence had learned the worth of cargoes, the workings and construction of ships, and how to take advantage of developing markets. They hoped to expand Rhode Island's share of trade within the British Empire, but events at home and abroad led to new challenges for anyone involved in the business of trade. The American Revolution was just over the horizon.

Chapter Four

First in Freedom: Rhode Island and the Revolution

By the 1770s, Rhode Island's population had grown to around fifty-eight thousand. There were approximately thirty villages and towns, stretching from Westerly in the southwest to Woonsocket in the north. Rhode Islanders were proud of their small colony's achievements and believed fervently in the freedoms guaranteed them by the 1663 charter.

Rhode Island was no longer an isolated outpost of religious dissenters. The colony's merchants had helped connect the colony to the other English settlements in America and to the rest of the empire ruled by Great Britain. Soon, events in America and in Great Britain would change Rhode Islanders' views of that empire.

The Sugar Act

From 1690 to 1765, Great Britain and its colonies were involved in four wars across two continents. The result was that by 1763 Great Britain was heavily in debt. The leaders of Britain's Parliament, not unreasonably, looked to the North American colonies to help pay for the empire's expenses. After all, the inhabitants were benefiting from British protection, British manufacturing, and British citizenship. Many in Parliament felt that since British citizens in Great Britain were expected to pay taxes, British citizens living in British colonies should pay taxes as well.

In colonial days, the most common kind of tax was usually directed at a particular industry or occupation and was designed to expire after a certain amount of tax had been collected or a certain number of years had passed. The Molasses Act of 1733 was one example of this type of tax. The act made it illegal for British ships to trade for molasses with anyone except the British possessions and imposed import taxes on any illegal trade. These taxes, however, had not been strictly enforced. Colonial traders, including many Rhode Island merchants, continued to trade with Spanish, Dutch, and French colonies in the West Indies in spite of the act's prohibition. And the merchants rarely had to pay any import duties, because the few tax collectors in Rhode Island were unable to inspect every ship that came into Narragansett Bay. So, Rhode Island ships brought home great quantities of molasses, which helped stimulate the economy, equalize the balance of trade with Great Britain, and provide income both at home and abroad.

The Molasses Act was supposed to expire after thirty years, and as the expiration date grew near, members of Parliament saw an opportunity to revise the act to create a new tax that would help pay off the war debts. The new act, the Sugar Act, was debated in Parliament throughout 1764. If passed, the Sugar Act would impose heavier import duties on molasses and other sugars from non-British possessions. Furthermore, these regulations would be strictly enforced through inspections by naval vessels.

Parliament also considered a Stamp Act, which would require a stamp to be placed on legal documents (such as wills, licenses, and school diplomas), newspapers, playing cards, and dice. The stamp showed that the manufacturer, publisher, or printer had paid a tax on the product or service. The tax would be paid directly to the government.

Colonists read the Stamp Act, a British law that imposed a tax on all paper products sold in the American colonies.

Stephen Hopkins Speaks Out

When Stephen Hopkins, the governor of Rhode Island, learned that Parliament was considering the Sugar Act, he wrote to the British Board of Trade to voice Rhode Island's opposition to the proposal. Hopkins pointed out that the passage of such a bill would be detrimental to the colony's commerce. He later wrote a pair of articles on the subject for the *Providence Gazette.* In November 1764, after the Sugar Act had been passed and the Stamp Act was still being considered, he wrote *The Rights of Colonies Examined.* This pamphlet is one of the first assertions of colonial rights over Parliamentary controls. In it, Hopkins wrote,

> [W]hat good reason can possibly be given for making a law to cramp the trade and ruin the interests of many of the colonies, and at the same time, lessen in a prodigious manner the consumption of the *British* manufactures in them? . . . Whatever burdens are laid upon the *Americans,* will be so much taken off the *Britons.* . . . And can it possibly be shewn that the people in *Britain* have a sovereign authority over their fellow-subjects in *America?* . . . In an emperial state . . . all laws, and all taxations, which bind the whole, must be made by the whole.[21]

Hopkins's work shows how the views of the American colonies had evolved since their founding. Originally, the colonies had been scattered English outposts on the edge of a continent, with little in common. But now the colonists understood that all thirteen colonies had common interests and desires. Hopkins's assertions that the colonists in America—not just in Rhode Island or in other individual colonies—were entitled to the same rights of taxation and trial by jury as the inhabitants of the British Isles presaged some of Thomas Jefferson's arguments in the Declaration of Independence more than ten years later. But Hopkins's protests, and the objections of other colonial leaders, were ignored in Parliament.

Enforcement of the Sugar Act

Rhode Islanders were appalled when efforts to enforce the Sugar Act began. British naval vessels patrolled Narragansett Bay with orders to stop and inspect any and all suspicious cargoes. In the colonists' eyes, Parliament added insult to injury by establishing an Admiralty Court in Halifax, Nova Scotia. This court could, without the benefit of a jury trial, try and convict anyone suspected of evading the Sugar Act levies.

Rhode Islanders were particularly outraged at this provision because the 1663 charter had allowed Rhode Island officials to establish

> the severall names and titles, duties, powers and limitts, of each court, office and officer, superior and inferior; and alsoe to contrive and apoynt such formes of oaths and attestations, not repugnant, but, as neare as may bee, agreeable, as aforesayd, to the lawes and statutes of this oure realme, as are conveniente and requisite, with respect to the due administration of justice.[22]

Rhode Islanders believed that this meant they were responsible for establishing their own courts and for establishing the English system of law, which guarantees a trial by jury. The Nova Scotia Admiralty Court seemed to ignore these rights. Rhode Island merchants, sea captains, crews, and civic leaders wondered how they could defend themselves in a court that obviously would be convened outside of the protection of Rhode Island's charter, even though the accused were charged within Rhode Island waters. However, Rhode Island, like the other colonies, had no representation in Parliament. Therefore, it had no means of lobbying for the repeal of the act and what it perceived as the act's infringements on Rhode Islanders' rights as British citizens.

"No Taxation Without Representation"

Parliament did not stop with the Sugar Act. It authorized other acts that Rhode Islanders found objectionable, including the Stamp Act, enacted in 1765. In 1766 came the Declaratory Act, in which Parliament asserted the right to legislate for the colonies whenever it saw fit, which of course would include imposing taxes. The Stamp Act was repealed shortly after it was passed due to a storm of protest on both sides of the Atlantic. Nevertheless, the colonists believed that Parliament and the Crown were endeavoring to

On June 9, 1772, Dudingston was chasing the sloop *Hannah* up the bay to search its cargo for contraband. The captain of the *Hannah* knew the bay better than Dudingston and, during the chase, lured the *Gaspee* so close to the shore that it ran aground on Namquit Point, a few miles southwest of Providence. Today, the point is called Gaspee Point because of what happened next.

In Providence, John Brown, the town's leading merchant, heard the news that the *Gaspee* had run aground. He knew that it would be several hours before the tide would come in enough to lift the ship off the point. Brown gathered some of his friends and employees to attack the trapped ship and, along with Abraham Whipple, one of his ship captains, volunteered to lead the assault. Around 2:00 A.M., eight longboats with muffled oars approached the *Gaspee* and were hailed by the ship's sentry. When the sentry got no reply, he summoned Captain Dudingston, who called out

A group of Rhode Islanders attack and burn the *Gaspee*. This act on June 9, 1772, was one of the first open acts of revolution against British rule.

into the night for the men to identify themselves. Whipple replied that he was the sheriff of Kent County and that he had a warrant for Dudingston's arrest. In the minutes that followed, one of the men in the longboats shot and wounded Dudingston, and the Providence crews swept onto the *Gaspee*, overwhelming its sleepy seamen. As its crew watched from their hastily launched longboats, the Rhode Islanders burned the *Gaspee* to the waterline.

Rhode Islanders still refer to June 9 as *Gaspee* Day and point to it as one of the first open acts of revolution against British rule. Dudingston recovered enough to file a protest with the British naval authorities. An inquest was convened, but no one was ever tried for the ship's destruction–despite Britain's offers of rewards for the names of the perpetrators. Rhode Island citizens refused to help the naval officials, who they saw more and more as representing a government that was ignoring its people in America.

A Call for a Congress

Over the next two years, Boston became the center of protests against British actions and resistance to British rule. Actions by "patriots," as those who were opposed to the British taxation policies called themselves, were met by increasingly harsh reactions by the British rulers. The Port of Boston was closed following the Boston Tea Party, in which angry colonists dumped British tea into Boston Harbor. The Massachusetts charter was declared null and void and British troops were sent to occupy the city.

These actions prompted the Rhode Island General Assembly to call for a Continental Congress to meet in 1774. This congress would include delegates from all of the colonies. Their purpose was to provide a unified colonial voice when petitioning King George for moderation in his government's actions and leniency toward those patriots accused of crimes during the protests. Rhode Island was the first colony to issue such a suggestion, and the first to elect delegates: Stephen Hopkins and his former political rival Samuel Ward. Even though tempers continued to flare, Rhode Island officials argued that all the colonies needed to unite to support each other's acts of civil disobedience. When the Continental Congress called for an embargo of all British

In what became known as the Boston Tea Party, colonists disguised as Indians dumped tea into Boston Harbor to protest British taxation.

goods, Rhode Island merchants endorsed it wholeheartedly. The time had come to put the colonies' welfare above their own individual interests. However, events were moving so swiftly that resolutions and declarations were soon replaced by open and armed resistance.

Revolution

Following the battles of Lexington and Concord in April 1775, Rhode Islanders joined their Massachusetts neighbors in the armed resistance to British rule. A thousand Rhode Islanders joined the patriot army for the siege of Boston; the first Rhode Islander to lose his life in the Revolution, Augustus Mumford, died from a cannon shot on August 29, 1775. In December 1775, 150 men joined colonial general Benedict Arnold, who marched to Canada to capture Quebec and to bring Canadians into the conflict on the side of the patriots. Their efforts were in vain, for they failed to capture the city and Canada remained loyal to British rule during the Revolution.

On May 4, 1776, the general assembly voted to dissolve its allegiance with the king of Great Britain. Although the vote did not specifically call for independence from Britain, Rhode Islanders interpreted the action as basically the same thing. May 4 continues to be celebrated as "Rhode Island Independence Day."

On July 4, 1776, the Continental Congress unanimously approved a motion called the Declaration of Independence that argued that the colonies as a whole needed to be independent from Great Britain. Rhode Island's two Continental Congress delegates signed the document without hesitation. Tradition has it that Stephen Hopkins said, "My hand trembles, but my heart does not,"[23] as he signed, attributing it simply to old age. William Ellery, who had replaced Samuel Ward in March 1776 after Ward died from smallpox, stood as close as he could to the congressional secretary in order to see the faces of the delegates as they signed. He later wrote,

On July 4, 1776, the Rhode Island delegates to the Continental Congress signed the Declaration of Independence without hesitation.

"By the Colony of Rhode Island and Providence Plantations. Passed by the General Assembly, May 4, 1776"

In response to the growing unrest in the American colonies, and Rhode Island's dissatisfaction with British rule, the Rhode Island General Assembly passed an act on May 4, 1776. The act is today seen as a declaration of independence from Great Britain. The following is excerpted from the full text of the act, which can be found in Samuel Greene Arnold's History of the State of Rhode Island and Providence Plantations.

AN ACT

REPEALING an Act entitled "An Act for the more effectual securing to His Majesty the Allegiance of His Subjects in this His Colony and Dominion of Rhode Island and Providence Plantations"...

WHEREAS ... George the Third King of Britain forgetting his dignity, regardless of the Compact most solemnly entered into ratified and confirmed to the Inhabitants of this Colony by his illustrious Ancestors—and 'til of late fully recognized by him—and entirely departing from the duties and Character of a good King—instead of Protecting is endeavouring to destroy the good people of this Colony, and of all the united Colonies by sending Fleets and Armies to America to confiscate our property and spread Fire, Sword and Desolation throughout our Country—in order to compel us to submit to the most debasing and detestable Tyranny whereby we are obliged by necessity ... to use every means ... in support of our invaluable rights & privileges; to oppose that Power which is exerted only for our destruction

BE it therefore Enacted by this General Assembly ... that ... an Act for the more effectual securing to His Majesty the Allegiance of His Subjects in His Colony and Dominion of Rhode Island and Providence Plantations be and the same is hereby repealed.

> I was determined to see how they all looked as they signed what might be their death warrants. I placed myself beside the secretary, Charles Thompson, and eyed each closely as he affixed his name to the document. Undaunted resolution was displayed on every countenance.[24]

The General Assembly endorsed the declaration on July 20, with a pledge to "Support the General Congress with our lives and fortunes."[25]

The Battle of Rhode Island

In December, barely six months after the Declaration of Independence, a British fleet sailed into Narragansett Bay and occupied Newport without firing a shot. They remained on Aquidneck Island for another three years, during which time half the population fled for safer areas. What had been a thriving shipping port and mercantile center became an armed encampment. The British roamed over the island at will, building fortifications against possible patriot action, recruiting citizens who remained loyal to the king, and taking whatever supplies they needed, such as food, flour, tobacco, and livestock. Unfortunately, there was little the Rhode Island government could do to remove the invaders. The Continental Army, under the command of George Washington, was more occupied with events to the south in New York, New Jersey, and Pennsylvania.

It wasn't until 1778 that Washington changed his mind, leading to the Battle of Rhode Island. Britain's traditional enemy, France, actively joined the patriot cause that year and sent men and supplies to support Washington's army. With the added resources from France, Washington decided in April that the British should be removed from Newport. He authorized General John Sullivan of Massachusetts to assemble eight thousand men for the attack, which would be made in coordination with a French fleet under Comte Jean Baptiste d'Estaing. D'Estaing and his men would invade Aquidneck from the southwest and Sullivan would invade from the north, along with troops from New York under the command of the Frenchman the Marquis de Lafayette.

General Washington and his troops travel toward the Delaware River to cross over to New Jersey.

In August, as Sullivan's troops moved onto the island, d'Estaing's fleet succeeded in driving the British ships from the harbor, only to meet another and larger flotilla that arrived on the scene. A storm wreaked havoc on both fleets, and the British sailed for New York for repairs. D'Estaing, ignoring his commitment to Sullivan, sailed for Boston. Thus, d'Estaing's forces did not invade Aquidneck Island as planned, and this may have made the difference in the American efforts to retake Newport. Even though Sullivan had driven the British back to the defenses around the town, he felt that without the additional French troops he was promised, his troops alone lacked the strength to capture it.

As the Americans retreated north, the British counterattacked. A short skirmish took place in Portsmouth, where Sullivan's troops withstood a furious assault and made an orderly retreat under fire. Rhode Island's black troops—black companies in the First Rhode Island Battalion, often called the Black Regiment—inflicted heavy

Nathanael Greene

When the Continental Congress appointed George Washington commander-in-chief of the patriot armies, it also appointed as brigadier general Nathanael Greene of Rhode Island. Greene's military genius helped the Americans win the war.

Greene commanded the Rhode Island troops during the siege of Boston in 1775–1776 before joining Washington's staff. He fought under Washington during the battles at Brandywine, Trenton, Germantown, and Monmouth before he was appointed to lead the Army of the South in 1780. His brilliant maneuvers against the British in the Carolinas exhausted his enemies. According to the National Park Service's *Guilford Courthouse National Military Park Official Map and Guide*, Greene summed up his southern campaign in one sentence: "We fight, get beat, rise, and fight again."

At Guilford Courthouse in North Carolina on March 15, 1781, Greene surrendered the battlefield to British general Lord Cornwallis and retreated into the countryside. Cornwallis suffered about 30 percent casualties, but Greene's army survived to fight another day. His efforts in the South cleared the British from Georgia and the Carolinas, and following the war the grateful citizens of Georgia deeded a large cotton plantation to him. Unfortunately, he did not live long after the war; Greene died of sunstroke in 1786 at the age of forty-four.

Greene's countrymen recognized his contributions to Rhode Island's and the nation's struggle for independence. According to *Rhode Island: A Guide to the Smallest State*, edited by Joseph Gaer, David Ramsey's 1789 "History of the American Revolution" proclaimed, "History affords but few instances of commanders who have achieved so much, with equal means, as was done by General Greene, in the short space of a twelvemonth. He opened the campaign [in the South] with gloomy prospects, but closed it with glory."

Nathanael Greene

losses on the British, but the Battle of Rhode Island can hardly be called a victory for the patriot cause. The British remained in Newport until October 1779, when they left of their own accord to join the fighting farther south.

Rhode Island saw no more land battles before the war ended, but Rhode Islanders participated in almost every major battle of the Revolutionary War. They suffered alongside soldiers from the other colonies during the privations of the Valley Forge winter, and the regiment under Captain Stephen Olney played a distinguished part during the siege at Yorktown that ended the fighting. With their newly won independence, Rhode Islanders could now turn to rebuilding their lives.

Chapter Five

To Ratify or Not to Ratify?

Following the conclusion of the American Revolution, Americans considered the country's future. After all, winning independence from Great Britain was one thing, but being able to keep the country as united in peace as it had been in war was another. For Rhode Islanders, the feeling of independence from royal rule in Britain was not new. It had been part of the colony's character since Rhode Island's founding. Now, as a state within the new United States, Rhode Island and its citizens had to determine what role they would play in the nation's future.

An Independent State

Rhode Islanders had made important contributions to the patriot cause and to achieving independence for the American colonies. However, "independence" meant different things to different people. To Rhode Islanders, whose tradition of religious tolerance and political independence dated back more than a hundred years, independence meant that everyone was free to go about his or her own business without interference from anyone or any government. Now that the British were no longer in charge, Rhode Islanders viewed themselves as belonging to an independent state, able to take care of themselves. Many wanted no part in any type of government that included all the former colonies.

The type of government the United States would establish was a matter of great debate among the nation's leaders. The words of the Declaration of Independence, proclaiming the right to life, liberty, and the pursuit of happiness, were lofty goals, but they were hardly a means of running a nation. The document had united the

The Declaration of Independence proclaimed the right to life, liberty, and the pursuit of happiness. However, these goals were not enough to run a nation.

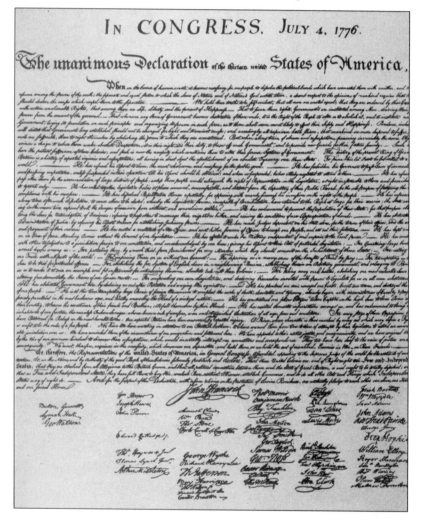

colonies by eloquently expressing the hopes, fears, and frustrations of the Americans who wished to be free from Britain. However, the Declaration of Independence provided no framework for governing the nation, nor did it address important issues such as electing representatives or a national leader. Congress tried to address some of these concerns with the Articles of Confederation.

The Articles of Confederation, enacted by Congress and adopted by all the states by the end of the Revolution, had joined the fledgling states into a single entity. The Articles' chief intent was to develop and pursue a coherent war strategy, and Congress was empowered to undertake that task. When the war ended, Rhode Islanders felt they should be able to leave the confederation of United States as voluntarily as they had joined it. After all, as the smallest state with the fewest natural resources on which to draw, Rhode Island had perhaps the greatest challenge in rebuilding after the war. Rhode Islanders turned their backs on the confederation of states, and although they continued to send delegates to Congress, they were determined to take care of their own needs first.

Life After the Revolution

The war had touched many people throughout the state. Many families had lost fathers, brothers, or sons to the fighting. Those who returned to rebuild their lives found that their children had grown up while they had been away. Many who had farmed the land had to plant crops and replace livestock that had been used to feed the armies. Merchants who had lost their ships to British guns or their crews to the American navy needed to rebuild both.

In some ways, the daily life of Rhode Islanders and their fellow Americans after the Revolution was much like it had been before the war. Homes reverberated with the tread of boots on wooden plank floors, and fireplaces throughout the house sputtered and hissed with burning logs. Echoes in the wind might carry the sounds of axes felling trees in the distance, or a hunter's gunfire, or a blacksmith's hammering. The gristmill's waterwheel creaked and groaned with the distinctive sound of wooden axles and

Moses Brown, Samuel Slater, and the Future

In 1774, Moses Brown formed a company with his son-in-law William Almy, and the firm of Almy and Brown started to take a keen interest in the new field of mechanical engineering. They became particularly fascinated by word of new British spinning and weaving machines that increased the production of yarn and cloth exponentially. However, England wanted to establish a monopoly in manufactured cloth, and the British government guarded the secrets of these machines closely. Exporting the machinery was forbidden, and anyone even remotely involved in its working was banned from emigrating from England.

In 1789, Moses Brown received a letter from Samuel Slater, who offered to help Brown build the English spinning machines. Slater had served as an apprentice to the co-inventor of the water-powered spinning machines, and he had learned every feature of the machines' intricate workings. Although the government banned anyone with Slater's expertise from emigrating, Slater had succeeded in leaving England, probably posing as a farmer.

With the financial backing of Almy and Brown, and the help of woodworkers and artisans in Pawtucket, just north of Providence, Slater reproduced the machine parts. After some trial and error, and careful examination, Slater succeeded in developing a facsimile of the system he had left behind in England. By 1791, the firm of Almy and Brown was offering manufactured cloth for sale in Providence.

Samuel Slater's spinning mill was the forerunner of the American industrial revolution. A process that had been time-consuming and could only be done by hand had been automated and was now being performed by water-powered machines.

gears. Women still had rooms set aside for weaving and spinning, where they taught their daughters the art of turning wool or flax into clothing. Men still tutored their sons in the art of cutting and stacking wood. Children still collected bayberries for candles, which an eighteenth-century writer described as giving off "a pleasant fragrance to all that are in the room."[26] A new generation learned the practicality of building the homestead so that its most used family rooms faced the south and its roof faced north. They learned how to place outbuildings such as barns, chicken coops, and outhouses relative to the house so that the prevailing winds carried offensive odors away, and planted herb gardens and honeysuckle so the same winds would carry their fragrances into the home.

In other ways, however, daily life for Rhode Islanders would not be the same again. Throughout the state, the character of communities had changed. Families who had remained loyal to the king had emigrated; many chose to live in Canada among other loyal British subjects. These loyalists took their skills and expertise with them, and in many cases, the communities they left behind could not replace them. The combination of lives lost through the war and the departure of loyalists hit the small state hard. The population of Rhode Island had been about fifty-eight thousand in 1774. Eight years later in 1782, it was only fifty-two thousand.

In Rhode Island, as elsewhere, the war had been a disaster for the schools. Private and community-run schools did not reopen after the war because teachers did not return to their former profession. Some were loyalists who left the country. Others who had gone off to assist the patriot cause had not survived the fighting or had decided to start a new life elsewhere. Rhode Island's schools had been few and far between even before the war; now, families concentrating on rebuilding their lives were too occupied with other concerns to be interested in reopening old schools or starting new ones. It was not until 1799 that the first law concerning public education was passed by the general assembly. That law was repealed in 1803 because representatives

Two citizens view the city of Providence. In some ways, life for Rhode Islanders remained the same, but the character of their communities had changed forever.

outside of the larger towns found public education too costly for their small communities. Finally, in 1828, the legislature provided permanent funding for public education in Rhode Island.

Changes in Trade

In a way, after the Revolution, Rhode Island's merchants discovered that they needed to go back to school. The nature of trade had changed with the war. Some merchants had stayed in business during the war as smugglers and privateers to help the revolutionary cause. Others, like the Brown brothers, had survived by helping provide the Continental armies with arms and munitions. Now that the war had ended, many tried to return to their prewar methods of filling their warehouses and serving their customers.

However, independence from Great Britain had brought unexpected changes to their livelihood. The merchants discovered after the war that being British subjects had carried certain advantages, such as protection by the British navy and a ready market in Britain and its colonies. Now that the United States was independent, it had no such benefits. Rhode Island and other American merchants found that all British ports were now closed to them in order to favor traders from colonies that were still part of the empire.

London had long been the center of commerce and banking in the British Empire, and Rhode Island merchants had regularly counted on London bankers to help them finance new ships, warehouses, and businesses. Now they found that these same bankers, who had been more than happy to extend them credit when Rhode Island was a British colony, would extend them no further credit. They also insisted that the Americans pay their debts. In response to this fiscal crisis, some Rhode Island merchants turned to trading centers elsewhere in Europe, such as in the Netherlands, France, and around the Baltic Sea.

Rhode Island captains and crews found that business in these parts of the world was filled with traditions and practices that were new and different, and they had to adjust. But slowly, the gambles began to pay off. From these new markets, Rhode Island ships began to import the British goods the American citizens wanted.

Among the gambles the Rhode Island merchants took, the one that became the most profitable was trade with China. One successful voyage of the Rhode Island ship *George Washington* provided merchants a tremendous incentive to outfit ships. In December 1787, the *George Washington* left Providence bound for China. The ship's cargo—anchors, ropes, sailcloth, rum, brandy, cheese, and candles, goods that Rhode Island manufacturers could easily supply—was worth $26,000. The ship was gone eighteen months; when it returned in July 1789, the cargo of tea, silks, cottons, lacquerware, and spices it carried was worth $100,000. This adventurous voyage had resulted in a substantial profit, and the sale of the new cargo brought money into the Rhode Island economy when it was dearly needed.

A Troubled Economy

By the end of the Revolution, Providence was becoming the center of the state's economy. The economy, however, was hindered by a lack of money. Rhode Island's government decided to face the money shortage in a way that had helped them in colonial days, especially during the imperial wars: It issued paper money.

Paper money was not commonly used in the eighteenth century; to most people, money meant gold and silver. Rhode Island's paper money system was developed by Jonathan J. Hazard, Daniel Owen, and John Collins. Their fiscal system was tremendously popular, and their "Country Party" controlled state politics from 1785 to 1790. The Country Party decided that the methods other states had chosen to pay off their war debts—

Providence was becoming the center of Rhode Island's economy by the end of the American Revolution.

imposing high taxes and accepting only gold or silver as debt payments—would only force many Rhode Islanders into greater debt. They believed that the well-being of the many was more important than repaying the rich who had invested heavily in the war effort.

The Country Party's paper money system was mainly designed to help the poor farmers of the state. The paper money helped the farmers rebuild their herds of livestock; pay off debts to suppliers, merchants, and tradesmen; and buy new seed for crops to help feed their family and the growing population. Rhode Island's richer citizens found that they had to accept the paper money from the farmers to collect even a part of what they were owed. The merchants would rather have been paid in gold or silver, because outside of Rhode Island, paper money was virtually worthless.

In additon, the paper became worth less than its face value because of a process called depreciation. For example, a paper note worth 50 cents was supposed to be exchanged by the state government for 50 cents in gold or silver. However, the total face value of the paper money the state had printed was more than the amount of gold and silver the state actually had. Merchants who turned in paper money had to accept less than its face value in order to get any gold or silver in exchange. In other words, a paper note supposedly worth 50 cents might, in fact, bring only 10 cents in gold.

The Country Party officials understood that depreciation was a problem, but they printed still more paper money. One Rhode Island author described the situation this way:

> [Paper money] had been issued at various times since 1710, the crisis coming in 1786 when the paper currency reached its greatest volume and also the lowest point in its depreciation. The legislature authorized in May a new issue of £100,000 and in June passed a supplemental act forcing creditors to accept the depreciated paper under a penalty of £100 and the loss of their right to vote.[27]

Rhode Island's paper money economy saved the state from upheavals such as Shay's Rebellion (shown here) in which impoverished farmers protested high taxes in Massachusetts.

The creditors might not have liked working with the paper money, but accepting it was better than the consequences of not accepting it.

This system frustrated many outside of the state. Out-of-state merchants who received Rhode Island paper money regarded it as worthless, as they could not use it in their home states to pay their own debts as they could with gold and silver. But the paper money system equalized the burden of Rhode Island's war debt among the rich and the poor. The poor were able to pay off their state taxes with the paper money at its full face value, and the state was able to use the paper money to pay off its creditors within the state. The system also saved Rhode Island from experiencing upheavals such as the 1786 Shays's Rebellion in Massachusetts, in which impoverished farmer-veterans staged an armed uprising in protest of high taxes.

Despite such protests, the nation's leaders continued to strive for a hard money solution to the country's debt. One proposal by Congress imposed a 5 percent duty on all imports to American ports to help reduce the war debt. Rhode Island delegate David Howell pointed out that the states had just fought a revolution that, in part, was in response to taxation by a central power. Rhode Island was already levying duties on imported goods, so Howell did not want his constituents to have to pay twice for the same goods. He proposed instead that the lands west of the Appalachian Mountains that had been ceded by Britain to the United States be sold to reduce the war debt. This was unpopular with many of the other states that had claims to those territories. All of this arguing in Congress led many to recognize the shortcomings of the Articles of Confederation, and prompted Congress in 1787 to revise the government under a new constitution.

The Struggle for Ratification

The new Constitution of the United States addressed many of the shortcomings of the Articles of Confederation. It called for a national leader, or president, to be elected for a four-year period. It also called for a congress that consisted of two bodies of elected officials: the Senate and the House of Representatives. Each state was allotted two senators regardless of its size; the number of representatives from each state was determined by its population.

Nine of the thirteen states needed to accept, or ratify, the Constitution in order for it to become the law of the land. New

Hampshire was the ninth state to ratify in 1788, making the Constitution the governing framework of the United States. Virginia, New York, and North Carolina ratified in 1789. Only Rhode Island was still debating the Constitution's merits.

Rhode Islanders objected to the Constitution as a basis for a national government for several reasons. Many were displeased with the Constitution's treatment of slavery. Rhode Island had passed a law in 1774 outlawing the further importation of slaves

George Washington in Newport, 1790

During the debates over ratifying the Constitution, George Washington had thrown his considerable political clout behind those in favor of the new document. Therefore, he found the opposition to ratification in Rhode Island particularly exasperating, and when he made a triumphant tour through the United States in 1789 after his election as president, he deliberately skipped the state.

However, Rhode Island ratified the Constitution in May 1790, and Washington made a trip there in August. During this visit, he sent an invigorating letter to the small congregation still worshiping at Touro Synagogue in Newport. The original letter, excerpted below, rests in the American Treasures of the Library of Congress, and can be found in full on the Library of Congress's website, "To Bigotry No Sanction." The letter remains a hallmark of the nation's commitment to religious freedom:

The Citizens of the United States of America have a right to applaud themselves for giving to Mankind examples of an enlarged and liberal policy: a policy worthy of imitation. All possess alike liberty of conscience and immunities of citizenship. It is now no more that toleration is spoken of, as if it was by the indulgence of one class of people that another enjoyed the exercise of their inherent natural rights. For happily the Government of the United States, which gives to bigotry no sanction, to persecution no assistance, requires only that they who live under its protection, should demean and had promised freedom to slaves who enlisted in the patriot armies (such as the men who fought in the Battle of Rhode Island). The Constitution, however, allowed the slave trade to continue until 1808, and it did not address freeing the nation's slaves at all. Other Rhode Islanders were reluctant to return to a government with an individual at the head. For them, the Constitution's office of president was different from the position of king in name only.

themselves as good citizens, in giving it on all occasions their effectual support.

George Washington

The debate over ratification dominated town meetings across the state. Then Congress voted to accept the Continental and state war debts at face value, agreeing to pay the states and citizens the full value of the gunpowder, arms, food, and other goods the nation had bought during the revolution. Rhode Island's wealthier citizens realized that if Rhode Island joined the other states in the federal union, under the Constitution they would be repaid the full value of the debts they were owed from the war. As a result, many of them started to voice support for ratification, voting in favor of it in town meetings in Bristol, Middletown, Portsmouth, Newport, and Providence. Providence officials even threatened to secede from Rhode Island and join the new republic on its own if the rest of the state did not vote for ratification.

However, the Country Party's paper money system still had many supporters throughout the state. In each of thirteen ratifying conventions from 1787 to 1789, the proponents of ratification lost. But slowly, the Country Party began to lose support. In May 1790, a convention of delegates from across Rhode Island assembled to debate ratification again. This time, ratification was approved—by a vote of 34 to 32.

Even this approval of the Constitution was not without debate. The convention delegates voted for ratification only with the provision that eighteen amendments be added to the Constitution to make it more appealing to Rhode Islanders' sense of religious freedom, tolerance, and spirit of independence. These eighteen proposed amendments were embodied in the ten amendments that today are called the Bill of Rights. Thus, Roger Williams's ideals of religious freedom and the separation of church and state became cornerstones of federal law.

The Spirit of Independence

Rhode Island's response to its money crisis following the Revolution meant that once again Rhode Island was seen as the home of rebellious dissenters. The only difference between the 1680s and the 1780s was that the Rhode Islanders displayed financial instead of religious independence. The state's use of paper money was neither bold nor innovative, for paper money had been used many times throughout the colonial period. But the Country Party's system helped as many Rhode Islanders as possible, and it helped ease the economic crisis in the state. Once again, Rhode

Pictured is the First Baptist Church in Providence. Rhode Island's insistence on religious freedom and separation of church and state became a cornerstone of federal law.

Island's leaders had chosen a path that was typical of Rhode Island's spirit of independence.

This spirit of independence also burned brightly during the debate over ratification. Eventually, Rhode Islanders in favor of joining the new federal union under the Constitution were able to demonstrate that the state's citizens did not have to compromise their traditional sense of freedom.

Epilogue

The Promise of Independence

As the nineteenth century began, Rhode Islanders and the entire nation looked to the future. With its new form of government defined by the Constitution, the United States was energized and optimistic. The spirit of independence that had been nurtured by Roger Williams, Anne Hutchinson, John Clarke, and others had spread through the English colonies. It had brought Americans from many different backgrounds and with many different beliefs together. Americans were proud of their accomplishments and were not hesitant to display their pride. American flags seemed to fly everywhere—in front of shops, schools, and homes, and on ships in ports far and wide. Albert Gallatin, Thomas Jefferson's secretary of the treasury, wrote that the nation was growing by leaps and bounds: "The energy of this nation is not to be controlled; it is at present exclusively applied to the acquisition of wealth and to improvements of tremendous magnitude."[28]

In Rhode Island, as across the country, the improvements took the form of better roads, better bridges, and better transportation networks from city to city. Entrepreneurs funded the building of bridges across the Providence and Seekonk Rivers, the Blackstone

This statue of Roger Williams overlooks Providence. Williams's spirit of independence spread through the English colonies.

Canal that linked Providence with inland Massachusetts, and railroads to link Rhode Island with Boston and New York. The American industrial revolution, sparked by Samuel Slater's woolen mills in Pawtucket, brought wealth to many and employment to many more.

For a time, the acquisition of wealth continued through trade with new ports of call. Every week, ships docked at wharves near

Providence after traveling to China, Portugal, Denmark, Sweden, or India. But starting in the 1820s, wealth came to those who exploited the state's natural waterfalls and built hundreds of water-powered woolen mills across the state. The success of Slater's mill eventually led Rhode Island merchants to change their focus from investing in shipping to investing in manufacturing, which in turn changed Rhode Island in the next century from a leader in trade to a leader in manufacturing. By the 1850s, Rhode Island investors were becoming wealthy from industries using not only the water-powered machinery of Samuel Slater but also the steam-generated machinery of George Corliss of Providence.

Throughout the nineteenth century, Rhode Islanders tried to stay true to the spirit of independence and equality fostered by the state's founders. A revised state constitution in 1843 was prompted by men like Thomas Dorr and Seth Luther, who championed the

The State House of Providence was designed to reflect the state's growth and optimism for the future.

rights of working-class citizens, many of whom were recent immigrants drawn to Rhode Island by the mills. This new constitution recognized that the state had changed since the charter of 1663. It removed the property qualifications for voting, thus enfranchising thousands of working-class citizens. It also redistributed representation in the general assembly so that the towns and cities had delegates based on their population. The constitution remains the basis of Rhode Island's state government today.

By the end of the 1800s, Rhode Islanders had endured a century of change and hardships. A new state capitol building was under construction in Providence to reflect the state's growth and optimism for the future. The architects' design called for a statue to stand atop the capitol dome. Rather than depicting Roger Williams, Thomas Dorr, or Samuel Slater, the statue, named the "Independent Man," represents all people—men and women of all faiths and races—who were drawn to Rhode Island and its promise of independence.

Notes

Introduction: Before the Colony

1. Quoted in Francis Newton Thorpe, ed., *The Federal and State Constitutions, Colonial Charters, and Other Organic Laws of the States, Territories, and Colonies Now or Heretofore Forming the United States of America.* Washington, DC: Government Printing Office, 1909. Available at Yale University's Avalon Project, www.yale.edu/lawweb/avalon/states/ri04.htm.

Chapter One: Beginnings

2. Quoted in Stuart O. Hale, *Narragansett Bay: A Friend's Perspective.* Narragansett, RI: NOAA Office of Sea Grant/University of Rhode Island, 1980, p. 29.
3. Patrick M. Malone, *The Skulking Way of War: Technology and Tactics Among the New England Indians.* Baltimore, MD: Johns Hopkins University Press, 1993, p. 46.
4. Malone, *The Skulking Way of War,* p. 10.
5. Quoted in William G. McLoughlin, *Rhode Island: A Bicentennial History.* New York: W. W. Norton, 1978, p. 7.
6. Quoted in Hale, *Narragansett Bay,* p. 31.
7. Quoted in Hale, *Narragansett Bay,* p. 27.
8. Quoted in McLoughlin, *Rhode Island,* p. 9.
9. Quoted in McLoughlin, *Rhode Island,* p. 36.

Chapter Two: A "Lively Experiment"

10. Quoted in McLoughlin, *Rhode Island,* p. 17.
11. Quoted in McLoughlin, *Rhode Island,* p. 38.
12. Quoted in Angie Debo, *A History of the Indians of the United States.* Norman: University of Oklahoma Press, 1970, p. 48.
13. Quoted in McLoughlin, *Rhode Island,* p. 44.
14. Quoted in Federal Writers Project of the Works Progress Administration for the State of Rhode Island, *Rhode Island: A Guide to the Smallest State.* Ed. Joseph Gaer. Boston: Houghton Mifflin, 1937, p. 28.

Chapter Three: Daily Life in the Growing Colony

15. Samuel Eliot Morison, *The Intellectual Life of Colonial New England*. Ithaca, NY: Great Seal Books, 1960, p. 70.
16. Quoted in Thomas B. Stockwell, *A History of Public Education in Rhode Island, from 1636 to 1876*. Providence, RI: Providence Press, 1876, p. 6.
17. Quoted in Alice Morse Earle, *Customs and Fashions in New England*. New York: Charles Scribner's Sons, 1901, p. 149.
18. Quoted in Earle, *Customs and Fashions in New England*, p. 158.
19. Quoted in Earle, *Customs and Fashions in New England*, p. 90.
20. Quoted in Hale, *Narragansett Bay*, p. 40.

Chapter Four: First in Freedom: Rhode Island and the Revolution

21. Stephen Hopkins, *The Rights of Colonies Examined*. Intro. ed. Paul Campbell. Providence, RI: Rhode Island Bicentennial Foundation, 1974, pp. 42–45.
22. Quoted in Thorpe, *The Federal and State Constitutions*, www.yale.edu/lawweb/avalon/states/ri04.htm.
23. Quoted in Donald C. Cooke, *Our Nation's Great Heritage*, Maplewood, NJ: Hammond, 1972, p. 28.
24. Quoted in Cooke, *Our Nation's Great Heritage*, p. 28.
25. Quoted in McLoughlin, *Rhode Island*, p. 94.

Chapter Five: To Ratify or Not to Ratify?

26. Quoted in Earle, *Customs and Fashions in New England*, pp. 125–26.
27. Quoted in Federal Writers Project, *Rhode Island*, p. 46.

Epilogue: The Promise of Independence

28. Quoted in Thomas C. Cochran, *Business in American Life: A History*. New York: McGraw-Hill, 1972, p. 61.

Chronology

1524
Giovanni da Verrazano sails around Block Island and into Narragansett Bay, becoming the first recorded European to visit what is today Rhode Island.

1591
Anne Hutchinson (née Marbury) is born in England.

1603
Roger Williams is born in England.

1614
Dutch explorer Adriaen Block visits the coast of Rhode Island and describes an island of red earth that he called "Roodt Eylandt."

1631
Williams, his wife, and his family immigrate to the Massachusetts Bay Colony.

1636
Williams, facing deportation for his views, flees beyond the claims of the Massachusetts Bay and Plymouth Colonies. He establishes a settlement at the head of Narragansett Bay and names it Providence.

1638
Hutchinson, her husband, and several followers found the settlement of Pocasset on Aquidneck Island. The settlement is renamed Portsmouth in 1643.

1639
William Coddington and others establish Newport. Roger Williams and others establish America's first Baptist congregation in Providence.

1643
Samuel Gorton and partners establish Warwick.

1644
The first charter from Parliament recognizes that the "Providence Plantations in Narragansett Bay" (Warwick, Newport,

Portsmouth, and Providence) constitute a colony separate from the other English colonies in the area.

1651
Coddington travels to England; Parliament grants his request to be named governor of Aquidneck Island. Williams and John Clarke travel to England to argue at Parliament that the four settlements should stay united and that Coddington's appointment should be revoked; they are successful.

1657
The first group of Quakers settle in Newport.

1658
The first group of Jewish colonists settle in Newport.

1662–1663
Clarke lobbies the king for a new charter for the Narragansett Bay settlements.

1663
A new charter granted by Charles II gives the settlements the official title "Rhode Island and Providence Plantations."

1675
"Praying Indian" John Sassamon is found dead in Massachusetts; three Indians are found guilty of his murder. King Philip's War begins with an attack on the village of Swansea. The Great Swamp Fight in southwestern Rhode Island results in the massacre of many Native Americans.

1676
Native American forces wipe out the English detachment at Central Falls, Rhode Island. Narragansett burn Providence. The war ends by the end of the year.

1683
Roger Williams dies and is buried in an unmarked grave near his original homestead.

1730s
Merchant trading companies in Rhode Island gain prominence.

1764
Brown University is chartered by the Rhode Island General Assembly as "Rhode Island College;" it holds its first classes in Warren, Rhode Island. Parliament passes the Sugar Act, calling for

greater taxation on the molasses trade and increased enforcement of regulations. Stephen Hopkins's *The Right of Colonies Examined* contends that taxation without representation is unjust.

1772
The British revenue cutter *Gaspee* is burned.

1774
The Rhode Island General Assembly calls for a meeting of colonial leaders in a Continental Congress to address common concerns.

1775
Rhode Island raises troops to assist the patriot cause in Massachusetts. Nathanael Greene is appointed commander of RI forces.

1776
The general assembly declares allegiance to George III null and void. Hopkins and William Ellery sign the Declaration of Independence. The British occupy Newport and Aquidneck Island.

1778
The Battle of Rhode Island; black troops in the First Rhode Island Battalion distinguish themselves in the fighting.

1779
The British occupation of Newport ends.

1785–1787
Rhode Island continues to send delegates to Congress but is uninterested in participating in the Confederation of States following the end of the Revolution.

1785–1790
The "Country Party" controls Rhode Island politics. The fiscal system developed by Jonathan J. Hazard, Daniel Owen, and John Collins, based on paper money, helps pay off the state's war debt shortly after the war's end.

1787
The firm of Brown and Francis sends the ship *George Washington* to China, starting a profitable trade for Rhode Island shipping firms.

1787–1790

Following Congress's adoption of the Constitution, twelve of the original thirteen states vote for ratification. Rhode Island holds thirteen ratifying conventions, but supporters of the Country Party continually rally support against ratification.

1789
Samuel Slater immigrates to New York and hears about Moses Brown and William Almy's experiments to reproduce the English woolen factory system. Slater travels to Rhode Island with his knowledge of the system and creates the first American woolen mill.

1790
Rhode Island votes to ratify of the Constitution but provides suggestions for amendments; these amendments become a basis for the Bill of Rights. President George Washington visits Touro Synagogue in Newport and reinforces the nation's commitment to religious freedom.

For Further Reading

Amy Allison, *Roger Williams*. New York: Chelsea House, 2000. A biography of the colonist who left the Puritan lifestyle and founded the settlement of Providence.

Avi, *Finding Providence: The Story of Roger Williams*. New York: HarperCollins, 1997. Avi presents the story of Williams's break with Massachusetts and the founding of Providence through the slightly fictionalized first-person narration of Williams's daughter Mary.

Scott Corbett, *Rhode Island*. New York: Coward-McCann, 1969. A thematic examination of Rhode Island history.

Leonard Everett Fisher, *To Bigotry, No Sanction: The Story of the Oldest Synagogue in America*. New York: Holiday House, 1998. This well-documented history of Newport's Touro Synagogue highlights individuals and events surrounding Jewish history in the New World and elsewhere.

Dennis Brindell Fradin, *Rhode Island Colony*. Chicago: Childrens Press, 1989. Fradin traces the history of Rhode Island to 1790 when it became the last colony to ratify the Constitution.

Judith Bloom Fradin and Dennis Brindell Fradin, *Rhode Island*. Chicago: Childrens Press, 1995. This book from the *From Sea to Shining Sea* series highlights people, places, and events and how Rhode Island fits in to the larger story of American history.

Olga Hall-Quest, *Flames over New England: The Story of King Philip's War, 1675–1676*. New York: E. P. Dutton, 1967. An interpretive work drawing heavily on first-person accounts of the war.

Ann Heinrichs, *America the Beautiful: Rhode Island*. Chicago: Childrens Press, 1990. This is a good introduction to the state, including a wealth of representative photographs.

Elizabeth IlgenFritz, *Anne Hutchinson*. New York: Chelsea House, 1991. This American Women of Achievement volume details the courageous life of the Puritan dissenter during the religious controversies of early seventeenth-century New England.

Joe McCarthy, *New England*. New York: Time-Life Books, 1967. An overview of the region's history and people.

Sylvia McNair, *Rhode Island*. Chicago: Childrens Press, 2000. Describes the geography, plants, animals, history, economy, religions, culture, and people of Rhode Island.

Eric Sloane, *American Yesterday*. New York: Wilfred Funk, 1956. One of several similar volumes by the author that brings pastimes, occupations, and ways of life from days gone by back to life.

Sylvia Thompson, *Rhode Island*. Austin, TX: Raintree/Steck-Vaughn, 1996. This book from the *Portrait of America* series discusses the history, economy, culture, and future of Rhode Island.

Edwin Tunis, *Colonial Living*. Baltimore, MD: Johns Hopkins University Press, 1999. Tunis examines the ways colonial Americans provided for themselves, including such essentials as food preparation and clothing manufacturing.

Margaret Dickie Uroff, *Becoming a City: From Fishing Village to Manufacturing Center*. New York: Harcourt Brace, 1968. Uroff documents the evolution of Providence from its founding to the twentieth century.

J. F. Warner, *Rhode Island*. Minneapolis, MN: Lerner, 1993. An introduction to the state's geography, economy, environmental issues, and interesting sites.

Susan Whitehurst, *Colony of Rhode Island*. New York: Power Kids Press, 2000. A history of Rhode Island for young readers (ages 5–9), from the arrival of the first Europeans to 1790.

Edna Yost, *Famous American Pioneering Women*. New York: Dodd, Mead, 1961. Interpretive essays documenting the contributions of some famous and not-so-famous Americans.

Works Consulted

Books

Elizabeth Anticaglia, *Twelve American Women*. Chicago: Nelson-Hall, 1975. A collection of biographical essays of American women from the seventeenth to the twentieth century.

Samuel Greene Arnold, *History of the State of Rhode Island and Providence Plantations*. 3rd. ed. New York: D. Appleton, 1878. One of the definitive collections of Rhode Island history in the seventeenth and eighteenth centuries.

John Braeman, *The Road to Independence: A Documentary History of the Causes of the American Revolution: 1763–1776*. New York: G. P. Putnam's Sons, 1963. A collection of abridged original documents from the American colonies and from Great Britain that traces the evolution of American calls for independence.

William Brandon, *The Last Americans*. New York: McGraw-Hill, 1974. A sensitive account of the Native Americans before the arrival of the Europeans.

Walter C. Bronson, *The History of Brown University 1764–1914*. Providence, RI: Brown University Press, 1914. The standard history of the Ivy League university's first 150 years.

Donald Barr Chidsey, *The Loyalists: The Story of Those Americans Who Fought Against Independence*. New York: Crown, 1973. An examination of several Americans who fought to keep the colonies under British rule.

Thomas C. Cochran, *Business in American Life: A History*. New York: McGraw-Hill, 1972. An examination of the interplay between business and society from the colonial period to the twentieth century.

Donald C. Cooke, *Our Nation's Great Heritage*. Maplewood, NJ: Hammond, 1972. Interesting biographical essays of the signers of the Declaration of Independence.

Cyclone Covey, *The Gentle Radical: Roger Williams*. New York: Macmillan, 1966. This biography of Williams's life until the 1640s examines in-depth his disputes with the Puritan leadership of Massachusetts and his relationships with the Indians of New England.

Burke Davis, *The Cowpens-Guilford Courthouse Campaign*. Philadelphia: J. B. Lippincott, 1962. Military historian Davis examines the pivotal campaign that drove the British from the South.

Angie Debo, *A History of the Indians of the United States*. Norman: University of Oklahoma Press, 1970. A social history of Indian-European conflict and cultural differences, including an examination of the changes in U.S. government policy concerning American Indians.

Alice Morse Earle, *Customs and Fashions in New England*. New York: Charles Scribner's Sons, 1901. Although the author concentrates heavily on the lives of Massachusetts Puritans in the seventeenth century, the book does provide a wealth of information on the lives of New Englanders during the early colonial period.

Federal Writers Project of the Works Progress Administration for the State of Rhode Island, *Rhode Island: A Guide to the Smallest State*. Ed. Joseph Gaer. Boston: Houghton Mifflin, 1937. This is primarily a travelogue designed for visitors to Rhode Island, but contains some fascinating tidbits of information about the state's cultural and natural history.

J. C. Furnas, *The Americas: A Social History of the United States*. New York: G. P. Putnam's Sons, 1969. Selected essays present views of the United States written by social historians and visitors to the United States.

Stuart O. Hale, *Narragansett Bay: A Friend's Perspective*. Narragansett, RI: National Oceanographic and Atmospheric Agency (NOAA) Office of Sea Grant/University of Rhode Island, 1980.

Thematic essays document the importance of Narragansett Bay in Rhode Island's history, economy, and future.

Oscar Handlin, *This Was America*. Cambridge, MA: Harvard University Press, 1969. A variety of essays from writers, diarists, and observers between the seventeenth and nineteenth centuries.

Stephen Hopkins, *The Rights of Colonies Examined*. Intro. and ed. Paul Campbell. Providence, RI: Rhode Island Bicentennial Foundation, 1974. Paul Campbell's introduction puts this important document in historical context, and presents biographical information to supplement the pamphlet's original text.

Paul Johnson, *A History of the American People*. New York: Harper-Collins, 1997. An examination of the development of the American character through the actions of the nation's leaders.

Patrick M. Malone, *The Skulking Way of War: Technology and Tactics Among the New England Indians*. Baltimore, MD: Johns Hopkins University Press, 1993. American civilization scholar Malone presents a remarkably balanced view of the art of war among Native Americans in New England, up to and including King Philip's War.

William G. McLoughlin, *Rhode Island: A Bicentennial History*. New York: W. W. Norton, 1978. A fascinating interpretive treatment of the state's history.

Samuel Eliot Morison, *The Intellectual Life of Colonial New England*. Ithaca, NY: Great Seal Books, 1960. A collection of essays documenting the variety of interests in literature and education in colonial New England.

——, *The Oxford History of the American People*. New York: Oxford University Press, 1965. Eminent historian Morison presents a one-volume history that covers a wide range of social and political issues that have faced the nation.

Gary B. Nash, *Red, White, and Black: The Peoples of Early America*. Englewood Cliffs, NJ: Prentice Hall, 1974. Nash reminds the reader that many contributions to the continent's history were made by non-Caucasians.

Eric Sloane, *Our Vanishing Landscape.* New York: Funk & Wagnalls, 1955. A primer on how to discover features of past uses of the land.

Thomas B. Stockwell, *A History of Public Education in Rhode Island, from 1636 to 1876.* Providence, RI: Providence Press, 1876. A parochial treatment of Rhode Island's early attempts at public education, with an emphasis on primary sources.

James L. Stokesbury, *A Short History of the American Revolution.* New York: William Morrow, 1991. Stokesbury condenses the Revolution into an easily accessible yet rather comprehensive one-volume work.

John Tebbel, *The Compact History of the Indian Wars.* New York: Hawthorn Books, 1966. A military history of Indian conflicts with Europeans and the U.S. Army.

Francis Newton Thorpe, ed., *The Federal and State Constitutions, Colonial Charters, and Other Organic Laws of the States, Territories, and Colonies Now or Heretofore Forming the United States of America.* Washington, DC: Government Printing Office, 1909. A collection of important documents from the nation's early history.

Chandler Whipple, *First Encounter: The Indian and White Man in Massachusetts and Rhode Island.* Stockbridge, MA: Berkshire Traveler Press. A slim volume that provides a history of the area up to and including King Philip's War.

Everett B. Wilson, *Early America at Work.* New York: A. S. Barnes, 1963. An interesting examination of vanished or nearly vanished occupations, such as lamplighters and sutlers.

Martha Zimiles and Murray Zimiles, *Early American Mills.* New York: Bramhall House, 1973. The authors examine water-powered mills from the seventeenth to nineteenth century, with a focus on the technology and architecture of the period.

Howard Zinn, *A People's History of the United States.* 20th ed. New York: HarperCollins, 1999. Insightful documentation of the country's history that reminds the reader that the nation was created by citizens other than male Caucasians.

Periodicals

Associated Press, "Narragansetts, Wampanoags Both Claim Harvard Remains," *Indian Country Today*, October 4, 2000.

National Park Service, *Guilford Courthouse National Military Park Official Map and Guide*. Washington, DC: Government Printing Office, 1986.

————, *Ninety-Six National Historic Site Official Map and Guide*. Washington, DC: Government Printing Office, 1984.

Internet Sources

American Treasures of the Library of Congress, "To Bigotry No Sanction (Memory)," August 30, 2000. www.loc.gov/exhibits/treasures/trm006.html

Avalon Project, Yale University Law School, "Charter of Rhode Island and Providence Plantations—July 15, 1663," 1998. www.yale.edu/lawweb/avalon/states/ri04.htm

The Jewish Student Online Research Center, "'*To Bigotry No Sanction, to Persecution No Assistance*'—George Washington's Letter to the Jews of Newport, Rhode Island (1790)," 2000. www.us-israel.org/jsource/US-Israel/bigotry.html

Office of the Secretary of State, State of Rhode Island and Providence Plantations, "RI History: RI Independence," 2000. www.state.ri.us/rihist/riindep.htm

Index

Index

Picture Credits

About the Author

Andrew A. Kling is a native of Providence, Rhode Island and has been fascinated with history for as long as he can remember. He began a career with the National Park Service by applying for a summer position in the Washington, DC area, and soon discovered he enjoyed interacting and sharing our nation's history with park visitors from all over the world.

Over the next 15-plus years, he worked for the National Park Service as a park ranger. His duties eventually included writing and editing a park newspaper, developing and presenting public programs, and from 1996 to 1999 planning and implementing visitor services associated with the relocation of the Cape Hatteras Lighthouse in North Carolina. He also co-wrote *Sea, Sands and Sounds: A Guide to Barrier Island Ecology and Geology*, a curriculum guide for middls school educators.

He is currently living in Montana where he works as a freelance writer and editor and interpretive media developer and consultant.